# the *Volkswagen* BugBook

the *Volkswagen*
# BugBook

*A Celebration of Beetle Culture*

By Dan Ouellette
Design by the Warren Group

ANGEL CITY PRESS

ANGEL CITY PRESS, INC.
2118 Wilshire Boulevard, Suite 880
Santa Monica, California 90403
310.395.9982
http://www.angelcitypress.com

First published in 1999 by Angel City Press
1 3 5 7 9 10 8 6 4 2
FIRST EDITION

ISBN 1-883318-00-9

*The Volkswagen Bug Book*
By Dan Ouellette
Copyright ©1999 by Dan Ouellette

Designed by Linda Warren and Laura Mische of the Warren Group, Venice, California

Portions of this book have appeared in the *East Bay Express* and the *San Francisco Examiner Sunday Magazine*

Photographs and images of Volkswagen advertising appear courtesy of Stiftung AutoMuseum Volkswagen, Wolfsburg, Germany;
Volkswagen of America, Inc., Auburn Hills, Michigan; and Arnold Communications, Boston, Massachusetts.

Disney characters ©Disney Enterprises, Inc. Used by permission from Disney Enterprises, Inc.

Excerpt on page 78 from *How to Keep Your Volkswagen Alive: A Manual of Step-By-Step Procedures for the Compleat Idiot*
©1997 reproduced with permission of John Muir Publications.

Library of Congress Cataloging-in-Publication Data
Ouellette, Dan, 1954-
The Volkswagen Bug Book : A Celebration of Beetle Culture
p. cm.
Includes bibliographical references.
ISBN 1-883318-00-9 (hard)
1. Volkswagen Beetle automobile—History. 2. Volkswagen automobile—History. 3. Automobiles—United States—History. I. Title.
TL215.V618 O84 1999
629.222'2—dc21
99-6082
CIP

*Printed in Hong Kong*

To Y-Bug with all my love.

— D.O.

# Chapters

# Bug**Contents**

**BugFiles**

Why write another book on the Volkswagen Beetle? That's the first question several people in the VW inner circle asked me when I began this project. It's been done before, so why bother again? I tried to explain that the book I envisioned had yet to be written. There are several mechanical manuals, a scattering of informative volumes on its history and a number of oversized photo books with dolled-up Bugs parked in front of fancy mansions. I was no more interested in beautiful Beetles than in engine specs or minor variations in body type over the course of the iconic car's history. What compelled me was how thoroughly the measly Bug bored its way into our lives. In a nutshell, I wanted to map the car's journey from its origin as the brainchild of a megalomaniacal world leader to its legendary role in twentieth century American culture.

Another question also arose: Why are you, a freelance music journalist and critic, writing about a car? Why not stick to your field of expertise and let a bona fide Bughead tackle the subject? Well, I'm not a fanatic about the car, but I *am* a Volkswagen Beetle aficionado. Since my senior year in high school in 1971, I have owned four Beetles, including a '74 that I still drive. I never assigned names to any of my Bugs, but get me going on the subject of the car and I can talk a blue streak about them as if they were old friends. In 1994 I wrote a sprawling literary nonfiction ode to the Bug for the Berkeley-Oakland weekly newspaper *East Bay Express* in which I not only expressed my passion for the car but also examined how the Beetle managed to worm its way into the fabric of American life. That article was the seed for this book.

To research this book and track down photos, I traveled to the source, to the Beetle's birthplace in Wolfsburg, Germany. At Stiftung AutoMuseum Volkswagen, Eckberth von Witzleben gave me the royal treatment by taking me on an informative guided tour and then graciously opening the photo file drawers to me. Von Witzleben, whose job it is to help researchers like myself, told me that one or two writers a year make the pilgrimage to the museum and factory. One such visitor staged an elaborate photography session with the museum cars, bringing in bright lights and expensive cameras to take stylized photos of the display models.

"I'm not interested in that," I said. "I'm more interested in your file photos of people enjoying the cars, painting them wild colors and making Beetle snow sculptures and sand castles."

"Oh, I see," Eckberth replied. "You want to capture the emotion of the car."

Exactly.

That's what I set out to do with *The Bug Book*, to exhibit the human-like characteristics of this personable machine that endeared itself to millions of owners and drivers.

An important note: *The Bug Book* has an unavoidable California bias. Although it once ranged far and wide throughout the U.S., the Beetle has virtually disappeared from the majority of America's highways. But it has maintained strong ties to the Golden State. The California connection continued with Beetle 2.0, which was officially born in southern California. In the early nineties, the Concept 1 prototype was conceived at the Volkswagen-Audi design studio in Simi Valley.

"Most car manufacturers have satellite design shops in California because of the unique lifestyle," says David Cole, a VW designer responsible for developing the new Beetle from concept who later became the assistant director of the car design program at the Academy of Art College in San Francisco. "Designers are allowed to dream more here, to conjure up new ideas that would never be appreciated in the regular design studios. A lot of new ideas are generated in California. Just look at mountain bikes and skateboards."

In the course of writing *The Bug Book*, three things happened. Almost everyone I knew or met smiled and offered encouragement. It was clear they had once known a Beetle. Plus, my appreciation for the car grew. Living in San Francisco and working in Berkeley, I see Bugs, no two alike, constantly. They're ubiquitous here. The funny thing is that they turn my head more than they ever did before. Then, finally, the new Beetle hatched. With it came many fond memories of its first cousin, which though it hasn't been sold in the U.S. since 1979, has definitely not been forgotten. A new wave of Beetlemania began.

*Dan Ouellette*
*San Francisco, 1999*

In 1938,
a *New York Times*
writer coined the term
"Beetle" for Hitler's new
car. Soon German's
called it *der Käfer*
(the beetle).

# love & lemons
# BugIntro

The Bug. A surprisingly simple, unpretentious name for a car that made such a profound and lasting impact. If you grew up within a three-decade span stretching from the fifties into the eighties, it's likely you've come into some contact with the Beetle. Even if you didn't own one or drive one, chances are you had a close friend who did. Volkswagen, the People's Car, lives up to its name. Its popularity cuts across race, nationality, gender, age and social class. Wherever two disciples are gathered, there's Bug church, a communion of air-cooled spirit, a camaraderie of four-cylinder experience, a festival of memories.

For many people the Beetle was their cheapo first car, the audition to driving life, the premiere performance on a clutch, the low-key, low-horsepower intro to motoring country back roads and frenetic freeways. Not much bigger than an amusement park bumper car, the Beetle felt like a trainer vehicle, a miniature version of a hunky Detroit-made four-wheeler, a trivial prelude to something bigger, stronger and more prestigious. Driving a Bug is fine for a youngster, but when it's time to grow up, it's best to be rid of childish pleasures, right? *Sure.* Welcome to the adult world of luxury vehicles: hefty monthly payments, expensive repairs and outrageous insurance premiums.

For other Vee Dub drivers, the Bug was the perfect second car, the errand vehicle, the around-town workhorse that didn't get the garaged attention or polished care the primary vehicle of the household received. It was the runt of the auto world litter, a stray given shelter, an orphan offered a home. Funny thing though, the Beetle often outlasted the glamorous model of the year and played the perennial second fiddle to several lead actors who each gradually faded into obscurity.

For the more adventurous types, the Bug was part toy, part indestructible beast that could entertain and delight for hours on end. It could be seen fearlessly plowing through ice-clogged brooks, squeezing down narrow wooded trails, churning through muddy fields, soaring over sand dunes, sliding and spinning on icy roads, bouncing off snow drifts and charging up steep rocky terrain that only trucks with four-wheel drive would dare traverse. As for those impromptu cross-country hauls, it was, hey, let's toss a couple backpacks and sleeping bags in the rear seat and go. If the engine explodes, the starter dies, the battery catches fire, well, let's do the Zen thing: deal with the inevitable breakdown in the Here and Now. If it means abandon ship and hitch for shore, so be it. In the meantime, let's rev 'n' roll.

For a select few, the Beetle became family. It was the favorite pet, the constant companion, the eager partner, the ready ear for road songs and highway confessions, the vessel that transported you through grief as well as elation. Most Bug owners named their cars, loved their cars, anguished over bidding them *adieu*. Freelance musician and publicist Susan Deneau in Los Angeles recently sold her 1978 Super Beetle convertible named Blanche. "The couple that bought her seemed like very nice folks and I made them promise to take good care of her," Susan said the day after she signed over the registration slip. "Nevertheless, I cried when they drove Blanche away."

Many Bug fans still have their cherished possessions, perhaps stored in the barn or on blocks in the garage, but more often they are on the road puttering away. For every Bug pockmarked and battered, there's one facelifted and cherried. Some Beetles, humbled and unassuming, are sans makeup, fully stocked with genuine Bosch parts. Others were fed horsepower steroids and have become super studs of the highway and racetracks. Still others have been transformed into works of art, whether with the glitzy, customized Cal Look (transforming the humble Beetle into muscular hunks and sex symbols) or by more imaginative means à la Harrod Blank's quirky moving sculpture car art, *Oh My God!*

The Bug evokes good memories. I had a new Beetle

Even if you didn't own or drive a Bug, chances are, you had a close friend who did.

on loan for a week from Volkswagen of America shortly before the company launched its latest model. The most unusual encounter occurred while parked on a quiet street in Marin County north of San Francisco. Two middle-aged gentlemen dressed in tweed jackets and ties approached me and asked if they could scope out the interior, the engine underneath the front hood and the hatchback. One of them immediately began to reminisce about an old yellow Beetle convertible he once owned and how he totaled it by accidentally ramming it into a brick wall. After ten minutes of genuine Bug gab, he suddenly remembered his real mission and produced a copy of *Awake* magazine. I politely passed on it, but thought, wow, even Jehovah's Witnesses are smitten by Beetlemania. Like everyone else in America, they too had Beetle stories to tell.

Most people I spoke to either owned one (my pumpkin Bug, purchased at a used car lot in 1978, is my third) or had some kind of memorable adventure in one. Whether it was learning how to drive a clutch on the steep hills of San Francisco, making out at a drive-in in the smallest, most cramped back seat imaginable or blowing an engine on the Bay Bridge and living to tell about it (my tale), Beetle lore is as American as apple pie and jazz. Not bad for a German-made car that is riddled with incongruities.

Ironically, the import that epitomized the nonconformist spirit of the late sixties and early seventies' love-and-peace counterculture in the U.S. was the offspring of Adolph Hitler's "motorize the people" campaign in the thirties. The vehicle of choice for eco-conscious hippies extolling its magical gas mileage in contrast to Detroit's petrol guzzlers, was in fact one of the most notorious air polluters on the road, an EPA *verboten* that hastened Volkswagen's decision to withdraw the car from the American marketplace in 1979.

If the Beetle does indeed have a soul, then it stands to reason that its personality should also have a shadow side. Its sweetness quickly turns sour when the topic of its Nazi

*Even under a blanket of snow, the Bug's distinctive profile is unmistakable.*

*Fill 'er up: a Bug got the royal treatment from four-wheeled attendants at a gas station in Deidesheim, Germany, in 1954.*

past is broached. And even Walt Disney Films' lovable Herbie the Love Bug had his cantankerous side when crossed.

On the mechanical plane, dependability represents only part of the Beetle story. There's a flip side to the coin. Certainly, a Bug love affair can last a long time, but you can be assured that at certain junctures the honeymoon will come to a screeching halt. Reality sets in and romance wanes when the cute Beetle, putt-putting along so smoothly a mile ago, suddenly sputters and shutters to a stop in the worst place possible: a dark, lonely highway deep in the country or smack dab in rush-hour traffic, much to the delight of fist-shaking, horn-blasting fellow commuters.

Or the Bug fails to wake up on the morning you have the most important job interview of your life. Then, the car becomes a curse, a despicable hunk of junk. Thousands of people made good on their threats to unload their lemons and buy a substantial car. (Yet, what percentage of those Bug traitors secretly wish they hadn't rashly sold their momentarily disabled cars?)

As for the new Beetle phenomenon, detractors deride it as just another stripe of *fin de siècle* nostalgia, a proliferation of romantic pining for a time when life was simpler, small was beautiful, the distinctions between allies and enemies clearer, and chocolate bars sold for a nickel a pop. Read: the late sixties, when all societal mores were up for grabs. It's not surprising that the Bug's peak year was 1968, when domestic sales reached a plateau at four hundred twenty-five thousand. (In 1972, Beetle number 15,007,034 rolled off the assembly line, thus establishing the model as the all-time auto champ, breaking the sales record held by Ford's Model T gas buggy.)

The Volkswagen Beetle defied the odds and became an American icon. The timeless old Bug still chugs along

The Volkswagen Beetle defied the odds and became an American icon.

the highways, even though its numbers are dwindling everywhere in the United States except perhaps in California, where it seems they all eventually come to roost.

Unpretentious and quirky, the Bug's reputation was built on a rare combination of factors. Foremost was its simplicity. It could even be worked on by the "compleat idiot," as proved by the late car mechanic-writer John Muir in his seminal "dummy" book, *How to Keep Your Volkswagen Alive*. The car also possessed humility. It made its mark as a David in the midst of Detroit's army of Goliaths. The Beetle was graced with reliability (despite their persnickety glitches and breakdowns, they do seem to run forever) and economy (cheap to buy, run and maintain). It didn't discriminate (the car attracted drivers of every race, age and gender) and served many functions (providing basic transportation as well as inspiring artists). Somehow the Beetle became much more than just a car.

The genius of the Beetle has always been that it appeals to a deep emotional desire to break out of the mold, to groove to a different beat. If the automobile had been popularized in the nineteenth century, Henry David Thoreau would have owned one. Back when thousands of the tiny blue-collar Bugs were scurrying around American highways, a few film actors championed the humble four-cylinder sedan, including part-time race car driver Paul Newman, who thumbed his nose at the trappings of stardom by spinning around Hollywood on Bug wheels.

At a time when our culture is increasingly homogenous and emulation is valued more than originality, these idiosyncratic cars plead a case for exercising one's freedom to be different, unconventional. With rare exceptions, most current car models, whether they're made in the United States, Japan or Europe, look eerily alike. But there's no mistaking a Beetle of any generation.

*Automotive writers road-tested early versions of the Bug on a German autobahn in 1939.*

As noted
in 1963 by
*Sports Illustrated,*
a Bug without gas
will float.

# *rubber soul* Bug Lore

**E**veryone has a Beetle story. That's because people didn't just own Volkswagens, they had relationships with them. As with all bonds, there were good days and trying times. Some of the family stories have happy endings, others tragic outcomes. Some anecdotes expound, others express whimsy. Bug lore teems with harrowing adventures and, on occasion, spotlights minor miracles. Courtships took place in steamy-windowed Bugs, wedding couples drove off on their honeymoons in Beetles and even babies were born in them (in the early days, Volkswagen of America handed out certificates to owners who gave birth in the back seat).

In the book *Small Wonder—The Amazing Story of the Volkswagen Beetle,* Walter Henry Nelson relates tales of the humble car's super-hero virility. He cites several accounts of Beetles being swept into turbulent river water after flash floods, floating to safety and saving the lives of all the trapped passengers. In addition to his "Floatswagen" stories, he recounts Bugs taking to sand dunes in Southwest Africa with the stamina of camels and withstanding grueling conditions in outback Australia. He also shares stories of flying Volkswagens, small aircraft propelled by factory-adapted VW engines. Then there are the heroics (not to mention trophies) of Beetles in nonstop marathon car rallies, some as long as fifteen hundred miles, in Africa and Australia. Nelson concludes, "A car which can float, fly and race engenders a great deal of loyalty, even of the sentimental kind."

Ah, yes, the romance with the ugly duckling. Rowland Nethaway, senior editor of the *Waco Tribune-Herald* in Texas, wrote a moving remembrance of the old Bug in response to the reports that Volkswagen was gearing up for Beetle 2.0. He recalled his father, a Ford lover, buying two Beetles in the fifties because they would last forever if cared for properly. As a teenager, Nethaway opted for the big, fast cars. However, when they broke down, he had to resort to borrowing one of his dad's Bugs

People didn't just own Volkswagens; they had relationships with them.

which "never failed to attract a crowd." He became a convert to the car that was simple, reliable and "practically indestructible." He wrote that his father was proved right by his Bugs, which both outlived him. Nethaway fondly noted, "I found out that those old Beetles would nearly last forever even if you didn't take care of them."

In true Herbie-the-Love-Bug style, two Volkswagen Beetles served as matchmakers for Lorrie and Bob Grimes of Antioch, California. In a weekly "Celebrations" section of the *Contra Costa Times,* the couple told how they met in 1978. Both drove nearly identical orange '71 Bugs, which as it turned out were purchased at the same car lot in the exact same month. The cars' license plates even shared the same three letters. They often mistook each other's car for their own. They finally met serendipitously and realized they had a lot more in common than their "junks." They got married and have been together ever since.

In a Bug celebration spread that ran in 1994 in the

*Springfield* (Massachusetts) *Sunday Republican,* several Beetle lovers inundated the newspaper with odes to the car. One couple recounted their adventures with a Bug when they moved to Guadalajara, Mexico. While there they drove all over the country as well as in Central America. Ronnie and Larry Field of Northampton, Massachusetts, reported that their Beetle went everywhere, through mud, sand and jungle—and even if they got mired, the car was so light the two of them could just push it to safety. As for a minor problem like losing their brakes in the mountains of Oaxaca, the Fields just took it in stride and drove one hundred miles in second gear until they reached a mechanic.

Another ex-Beetle owner remembered her first car, a '59 black Bug called "The Percolator." Another Bughead complained about the lack of heat in his '73 fluorescent orange Beetle, yet admitted that he bonded with this car more than any other he's owned. There were tales of packing in friends and going to hippie concerts, resorting to the

*The intrepid Beetle dubbed "Antarctica 1" hits the snowy trail on the bleak continent in 1963.*

# Beetles to the Rescue

*I* did everything wrong when I bought my 1968 Bug convertible. I paid too much, I didn't get it checked out by a mechanic, I overlooked little details like no seat belts. I just fell in love. It was beautiful. Cherry red with a black top and black interior. Everything that could shine on it did. There was chrome on the engine and a pair of twelve-inch speakers on the rear deck so I could blast my music when I cruised up the coast.

When it was running right, it was the perfect place to be on a warm southern California day. Unfortunately, there weren't many days when its engine cooperated. A few months in, little things started to go wrong. First the brakes, then the clutch, then a little oil leak which turned into a big oil leak which turned into a spark plug that didn't quite stay in. The car never completely died on me. It always started up if I gave it a few minutes to rest. But I didn't always have a few extra minutes and my frustration mounted.

I finally opted for the big-ticket item—a new engine. I figured all my problems would be solved, and for a while they were. But there were a few things I hadn't yet learned about Bug ownership. The most critical was about the fuel line having a tendency to rot.

One summer night on my way home from work, I got off the Santa Monica Freeway at Centinela. Just short of Ohio Avenue, I stalled. This was not a new experience for me. After all, I'd driven the car on two cylinders before. I started it up and it stalled again. I got it started once more and then I heard a backfire like I'd never heard before. It shook my guts more than the twelve-inch speakers.

I looked in my rear-view mirror and saw flames leaping up. My response was the only logical one—I exited the vehicle, slammed the door, walked to the rear and started beating the car with my briefcase (not that it would help, it just made me feel better).

In a matter of what must have been only seconds, three other Bugs appeared in the intersection. Their drivers all produced fire extinguishers and attempted with some success to beat back the flames consuming the convertible top. I retired to the curb to fret when a Porsche pulled up and its driver produced a Halon extinguisher that snuffed the fire out in one puff of chemicals.

As Centinela Avenue is the dividing line between Los Angeles and Santa Monica, I was honored with the presence of both fire departments. One Santa Monica fireman offered me fifty dollars for the remains, but I foolishly insisted that AAA tow the hulk to my home, where it remained for the next year. It served as a part-time homeless shelter until I finally sold it to someone else for fifty dollars.

I still dream of that car.

— Erik Filkorn

use of a screwdriver to start the car and applying pink contact paper cut into stars on a black Bug crunched in an accident. But the best story came from a bright yellow '79 Bug owner, C. Maroney of Springfield, Massachusetts, who looked out the window while driving to see a bright yellow canary flying alongside. "I think he thought my Bug was his mother," Maroney wrote.

In addition to stories about Bug good times, there are the tales of scoring great deals. Yunus Peer is a bona fide Beetle fan whose parents' first new car was a '62 Bug. Originally from South Africa, Peer moved to New Hampshire in 1985 to work as a teacher at Proctor Academy in Andover. His goal when he arrived was to find an old Bug—not an easy task at the time since most Beetles in that area had expired years before. But soon he spotted a beauty, a blue '67 Beetle that an elderly woman with white hair drove around town. Peer approached her one day and inquired about her car. The woman snapped back at him, "Young man, forget it. I have four grandsons lined up waiting for this car."

*Bug meets buggy.*

A couple of years later Peer saw her again and walked over to her. Before he could say a word, the woman said that she remembered him and to not bother even asking her about the car. In 1991, Peer asked a pump attendant at the local gas station to be on the lookout for a Beetle. He had just restored a '73 Bug and was restless to begin work on another project. The attendant told him he knew exactly where one was and directed him to a barn down the street. Peer went there and found the blue Bug the elderly woman owned. A year earlier she had broken her hip and was forced to stop driving. Her grandsons were scattered all over the country and her son-in-law was eager to get rid of it. The seats were brand new and the odometer read fifty-nine thousand miles. She just drove the car to church on Sunday. He bought the Bug for seven hundred fifty dollars.

For Peer, there's also the flip side of the coin: selling a Bug to just the right party. He purchased a red '65 convertible with a white top from an antique dealer who had once vowed to never sell the car. He called Peer one day and said he had a change of heart. Peer bought it, worked on it, then decided to sell it a few years later. He put an ad in the *Boston Globe* and his phone immediately began to ring off the hook. He fielded the calls and made notes about prospective buyers.

The most interesting offer came from a lawyer in Manchester, New Hampshire, who was planning a combined birthday and wedding anniversary party for his wife. He told Peer, "On our wedding day, we drove from the church in a red '65 convertible. I want to surprise her with the car." Peer replied, "It's yours.

You deserve it. I know you'll appreciate it more than anyone else." Peer delivered the car while the lawyer's wife was off taking a jog. The lawyer parked the Bug in the driveway with a bouquet of flowers on the seat and no doubt got the weekend celebration off to a great start.

Other Volkswagen owners tell their stories with so much passion and love that they personify their cars, instilling them with an entire range of emotions from joy to jealousy. Case in point: Lois Grace, historian of the Vintage Volkswagen Club of America, Golden Gate chapter. Her VWs have become integral members of her family. Her children include her first love, Vernon, a '59 Type II Transporter bus; Oscar, a '58 convertible Bug; and her

*Frat boys mugged in a "Bug cram," left. Multipurpose Bug braved snow drifts, above.*

"daily driver" Bogart (a.k.a. Bogie or Humphrey), a '69 Beetle. Lois has written dozens of stories in her own personal missive, the *FRAUline*, as well as the national club's newsletter, *The Autoist*.

Instead of dramatic adventures or tall tales, Lois' lore has more in common with a photo album or home movies. She writes, "Many VWs (like my own Vernon) have been in families for years and it's fun to tell spectators about the 'family history' of the car." So she relates tales about cleaning engine crud, doing "the brake job from hell," entering her babes in beauty contests, breaking down on the highway, taking road trips and getting in crashes.

On the topic of spiffing up Vernon, Lois writes, "This must be how our favorite dental hygienist feels when faced with a patient who hasn't flossed in thirty years. There were bars, and pins, and bolts and nuts, and things everywhere, but the most intimidating part about it all was that the entire set-up was covered with about a foot of grease and dirt."

After an embarrassing (for Vernon, not Lois) breakdown, Grace reports that the bus was happy to be home from the shop, healthy once again. "His new fuel pump looks wonderful and, more importantly, works perfectly. I drove Vern home and got him back inside the garage, ready for his next outing. I think he just needed that new pump to be sure he was still

*Bug as tractor kicked up some dust, left. Big man lifted small car, strings attached, above.*

Recalling bug tales accounts for more than party chit-chat. The stories stand for fellowship and communion.

my favorite. I can't be too hard on the old guy. I think he's still having trouble adjusting to a sibling. He's thirty-two years old and has just now gotten a baby brother. Oh, well, I think Vern knows he'll always be my first-born!"

Don't try telling Lois Grace her Volkswagens don't have souls.

Art and simplicity: that's how Cincinnati Bug lover Paul A. Klebahn describes the Volkswagen Beetle. He's owned fourteen in various conditions over the course of his life, so he has his share of stories. He loves to tell them, and he loves to hear fellow Bug owners' tales as well. In fact, he started collecting stories as a hobby in 1991. Working in a professional sales position, Klebahn came into contact with a range of people, from secretaries to CEOs. Because he was such a Bughead, the subject of VWs inevitably came up. In the back of his mind he thought that someday he'd like to compile all the stories into a series of Bug tale books.

Little did he know then that seven years later, he'd have his first book, *Bug Tales*, ready to go to press along with a Bug Tales web site and interview appearances on the *CBS Evening News* and National Public Radio. The project took on a life of its own as people from as far away as Egypt and Australia either e-mailed or telephoned in their stories.

One of Klebahn's earliest memories was a red '61 Bug with a white leatherette interior. The car was his parents' only means of transportation at the time of his birth. His accountant father bought the car in 1962 and upon Paul's arrival in 1964 removed the back seat and replaced it with a makeshift playpen. "As I recall, this was a particularly fun feature during evasive traffic maneuvers," Klebahn writes of his own experience in *Bug Tales*. "Today this probably accounts for my near perfect impersonation of a pinball."

Sadly, the Bug-smitten Klebahn notes, his parents soon traded in the Bug for a heftier family car, a Dodge Coronet. He had to settle for Matchbox VWs until he came of driving age. Then he and his father went "Bug hunting"

# High & Unusual Places

*T*ravel writer Eric Hansen, who has written the books *Motoring with Mohammed* and *Stranger in the Forest,* has seen his share of Beetles in strange places in his wanderlust jaunts. The most remotely situated Beetle he ever saw was in 1972 in the mountains of north Pakistan where the car was revered by locals for its stamina.

High-tech high priest John Perry Barlow, best known for appropriating the sci-fi word "cyberspace" to describe the milieu of the Internet, recalled a time when he took a spiritual journey to the Himalayas in search of wisdom. As might be expected, Barlow crossed paths with a Tibetan monk. Barlow thought the mystic was talking in parables when he asked him about car mechanics. However, the sage really had specific questions about getting his Volkswagen up and running. Barlow's epiphany: don't take things so seriously.

In 1962-63, a ruby red Beetle, built in Australia, spent a year in Antarctica at an Australian scientific site called Mawson Station. Dubbed the Red Terror by the scientists and Antarctica 1 by Volkswagen, the car survived hurricane-strength winds, massive snow drifts and steep terrain impassable by dog teams. After its term of duty was over, it was replaced by another Beetle, Antarctica 2. A few years later Antarctica 1 won the BP Rally, a grueling two thousand-mile backroads race in southeastern Australia.

and bagged a fixer-upper black '74 Super Beetle. The two were pleased with the purchase even though they didn't see eye-to-eye about its function. "[My dad] saw a Spartan economy car whereas I saw a blank canvas," Klebahn writes. "It didn't take long before the '74 Super was completely customized, named California Fever and winning trophies at shows. I don't know whether it was the Porsche wheels, whale tail, louvers, etched glass or custom paint, but one thing was for certain: it clearly was no longer basic transportation."

Thus began Klebahn's love affair with Volkswagens of all varieties, including Karmann Ghias, busses and convertibles. However, in his senior year of college, he reluctantly sold California Fever to make ends meet. Several years later his wife Gretchen, enamored of air-cooled VWs, insisted on renting a brand new Beetle in Mexico (where the cars are still made) during their vacation.

Like all Bug owners and drivers, Klebahn discovered that nearly everyone has a Beetle story. It doesn't matter whether you owned one or drove one or simply hitched a ride in one, the experience was indelible. Recalling Bug tales accounts for much more than party chit-chat. The stories stand for fellowship and communion.

●

*Tourists in Wolfsburg, home of the Bug, rode on the 1958 Bug train. Maximum speed: six kilometers per hour.*

# Oscar Arrives

We had a Blessed Event at our house recently, but the "baby" weighed in at over eighteen hundred pounds, took me home that night and is already thirty-two years old. The Perfect Child, I'd say. My newest boy, Oscar, arrived a month ago. He's a 1958 Bug convertible. He's black with a black top, and for his age is in remarkably well-preserved original condition. His arrival changed a few things within our family, as new babies usually do.

*Lois Grace, middle, and her siblings posed with dad's cool car on Easter morning 1957.*

My '59 single cab Transporter Vernon has been my first love for as long as I can remember. I've always had a weakness for the Type II BusFaces. My daily driver, Bogart, is a wonderful little fella, but he's new. He's a 1969 model, and while not what you'd call the latest, he's still new when you're talking in terms of Vintage VWs. So, Oscar was a bit of a shock. Unlike Vern, the steering wheel isn't flat. He has a back seat. The gas filler is under the hood. He drives like Vernon but is shaped like Bogart. And, strangest of all, he can actually flip his lid.

When Oscar smiled at me, I smiled back, but I wasn't sure he was the one. Nevertheless, I called about him that night and drove him the next day. I wasn't radically impressed—his muffler leaked like a sieve and his steering felt like it was connected with rubber bands. The brakes were mushy. He had no taillights—they had been stolen after Oscar had been sitting out for sale for one day. Heck, he only had one license plate. But there was something there that called to me. He looked at me as if he were hoping I'd want to take him home. It had been a while since anyone cared about him. Sure, his owners had done all the right things, more or less, but no one cared. Pretty soon, I stopped making excuses and I bought him.

How did he become Oscar? Well, he needed a name, that much was obvious, and after all, he is an older gentleman who wears a black toupee, so we had to be careful. "Dudley" came to mind. But, the day after he came home I went out to greet him, and Oscar looked back. It was that easy. His name proved to be comical, yet dignified. He seems happy with it. Vernon and Bogart tried to make him feel welcome, but I think Vern in particular was a bit bewildered. He was used to being the only Vintage Beast in the house, and this new one didn't even have a roof.

Convertibles are funny. They love attention. The first day I drove Oscar someone wanted to buy him from me at a stoplight. It seems as though you are more visible in a convertible. It's almost a state of mind. You're sitting right out there in the wind and the sun and the smog. Everyone around you can hear your radio. Birds talk to you as they fly over. Smells are more potent. The sun is warm on you but the breeze is cool. Riding in Oscar is more like being on a roller coaster than driving a car.

— *Lois Grace*

*For a Beetle lover, no birthday is complete without a Bug ride, right.*

**2**

The "28IF" license plate of the Beetle shown on the cover of the Beatles' *Abbey Road* album was an important clue in the "Paul is dead" mystery.

# BugCelebs

*stars on wheels*

The enormous appeal of the Volkswagen Beetle is that it so soundly defies pretension, privilege and prestige. In the true sense of its heritage, it is the People's Car, the auto of the masses. In its heyday, it was favored by students on minuscule budgets, families in need of second cars, poor folks down on their luck. Bug drivers may have admired fancy cars from afar, but those luxury liners were strictly look-don't-touch means of transportation. The Beetle was totally hands-on.

Even though it was the commoner's car of choice, the Bug also had its devotees in high places. In Hollywood, where image is god, the lowly Beetle didn't stand much of a chance amidst stretch limos and jazzy sports cars. Drive a Bug and kiss that career as leading man or lady good-bye. Yet because the car was so odd and small and lowly, a few select high-profile personalities tooled around in them as an act of defiance against the culture of ostentatious consumption.

Perhaps the earliest and most famous big-star Bug owner was Paul Newman, renowned in later years for his socio-political activism ranging from his protest against the Chinese government's persecution of the Tibetan people and their spiritual leader the Dalai Lama to his Newman's Own food company, which donates profits to charitable organizations. While Newman pursued auto racing as an avocation, he also drove a 1963 Volkswagen Beetle. Even though it was powered by a Porsche engine and transmission and enhanced with other high-performance features, Newman made a statement against the posh Hollywood mindset by driving it when he lived in Beverly Hills.

One evening Newman and his wife Joanne Woodward attended a gala black-tie party held in honor of Britain's Princess Margaret (also a Beetle owner of prominence). They drove to the event in their Bug. After the bash, while the large crowd of affluent attendees waited for their cars to be delivered by the valet parking staff, the conspicuous '63 Beetle arrived and the tuxedoed Newman and evening-gowned Woodward climbed in and spun off. While some uppity partygoers were no doubt aghast at the Bug mingling with their Rolls-Royces, Ferraris and Lincoln Continentals, the Newman mystique inspired many gatherers to break into spontaneous applause for his Bug boldness.

While the Beetle stood for social insurgency, it also served as a comedic device, a straight man of sorts. Comedian Bill Cosby knew that the audience for his stand-up routine would roar with laughter when he described his adventures on the hills of San Francisco driving a friend's borrowed Bug. On his 1965 comedy album *Why Is There Air?* (Warner Bros.), Cosby recounts his driving experiences there, zipping around town and actively avoiding the "straight-up and straight-down" streets best left to cable cars. However, Cosby is forced to take a detour that leads to one of the steepest hills in the city.

Voicing blubbery, close-mike sound effects, Cosby emulates the Bug's distinctive puttering as he guns the motor to soar up and over the incline unscathed. The hitch? A stop sign at the crest. He's caught, so he slams to a halt, then has to coordinate the clutch, brake and accelerator to make it to safety. He fears the worst: flying backwards at breakneck speed into the Bay. "And if you die that way," Cosby jokes, "they won't let you into Heaven." St. Peter at the Pearly Gates asks for the cause of death, Cosby responds, "Me and a Volkswagen drifted backwards into the Bay," and St. Peter pronounces his judgment, "You go to hell."

Liberace also got mileage out of the Bug, using it as a visual joke. In his Las Vegas act, the flamboyant pianist made his grand entrance, chauffeured in a mirrored Rolls-Royce. After flaunting his latest outfit, he'd take off his robe and be at a loss as to where to put it until a mirrored Beetle with a Rolls-Royce grille arrived on stage. While the audience howled with laughter, Liberace deposited his cape into the Bug, which then returned to the wings until the next show.

The Bug strikes a chord with comedians. Maybe it's because the car itself is funny to look at, maybe because the

runt of the auto industry lent itself so easily to being the brunt of jokes. It's been suggested that the Bug is best suited for clowns. But Jerry Seinfeld, inarguably the hottest comedian of the nineties and an avid car collector, is a Beetle fan for entirely different reasons. Seinfeld's fascination with Volkswagens comes from his experiences as a youth. He grew up in Massapequa, Long Island. His father owned a shop called the Kal Signfeld Sign Company and used a Volkswagen Transporter to carry his wares. The future sitcom star learned how to drive by grinding the gears on that van.

After Seinfeld graduated from Queens College in 1976, he took the stage at the Comedy Club in Manhattan, fell flat on his face, went back to the drawing board to rejigger his stand-up routine, then triumphantly returned three months later. He went on to become the emcee at the Comic Strip in New York, marking the beginning of an immensely successful career as comedian and television star. Years later, Seinfeld commemorated his breakthrough as a joke-teller by purchasing a convertible Beetle, built in 1976, the same year his jokes began to pay off (he's since sold the car).

While Seinfeld is a car buff with a penchant for Porsches (his entire collection is housed in two airplane hangers at the Santa Monica airport), he also owns a multi-windowed blue and white '64 Volkswagen van, no doubt in homage to his late father, and a 1966 green convertible Bug, which he bought from a guy in Wisconsin who was storing it in his barn. When he purchased the latter, it had only one hundred and seventy-five original miles on it. To score this prize, Seinfeld outbid Volkswagen itself, which wanted to buy the car for its own collection.

With a reputation as a Beetle fan, Seinfeld was contacted by *Automobile* magazine in 1994 and asked to play the role of guest car correspondent. His assignment? Scope out the top-secret new Beetle, then known as the Concept 1 car. He gave the prototype an enthusiastic thumbs-up. He

*Blues-pop singer Eric Clapton takes a break with Mona Lisa, during a 1998 European tour sponsored by Volkswagen.*

# Big Names Pitching Little Cars

Comedian Jimmy Durante, who made a career out of big-nose jokes, sits in a brand-new 1973 Super Beetle and announces, "They finally made a car big enough for Durante." And, he says, there's extra room for the old schnozzola. He sings a bit of his "Ink A Dink A Do" theme song, then happily finds himself joined in the car by three beautiful women. He smiles and says the new extra-sized Beetle has plenty of room for companions.

Zsa Zsa Gabor touts a metallic blue sunroof Beetle, available in a Limited La Grande Bug edition.

McLean Stevenson, better known as Lt. Col. Henry Blake from the TV series *M*A*S*H*, appears in two commercials. In one he's selling a 1949 Packard, a monstrosity of a car, at a 1949 auto show, which also featured other U.S.-made boats surrounded by large, cheering crowds. No one attends the Volkswagen sales pitch. Several years later, the commercial points out, only the humble Beetle remains. In a humorous commercial pushing the 1971 model, Stevenson with microphone in hand at a dealership, announces the ceremonious arrival of the eighteen millionth Beetle customer, a guy who turns out to be there only to deliver a tuna-on-whole-wheat sandwich.

Apollo astronaut Edward Eugene "Buzz" Aldrin touts the new 1972 Volkswagen's computerized service system as being almost as sophisticated as the NASA technical system that had allowed him to walk on the moon three years earlier.

appeared on the cover of the May 1994 issue in front of the yellow car, holding a black-and-white ad image of the old Bug and making a goofy face. Reportedly, he hated the shot and angrily distanced himself from the story. Although Seinfeld scoped out the new Beetle when it first appeared, he didn't buy one. For the final episode of his *Seinfeld* television program, a "newby" Beetle was scheduled to make a cameo appearance. However, in a last-minute script revision, the car was cut.

Other Hollywood notables could spin a tale or two of their own Bug days. Actor Clint Eastwood drove one. Super model Cheryl Tiegs bought a blue Bug as her first car (it was stolen, so she replaced it with a new SL280 Mercedes convertible). Actress Gillian Anderson, best known for her role as FBI Agent Dana Scully in *The X-Files*, remembers growing up in north London and riding in a Beetle with her financially-struggling parents (they moved there when she was two and settled in for nine years before returning to the U.S.).

Not every famous Bug owner is nice. It was the car of choice for notorious cult leader Charles Manson. He instructed his "family" of followers to steal them off the streets of southern California and remake them into all-purpose dune buggies in preparation for the Apocalypse, which he predicted was just around the corner in the late sixties. Like Hitler, Manson saw the benefits of the air-cooled, rear-engine Bug. He envisioned the car maneuvering through the desert terrain of Death Valley where he and his faithful band of mass murderers planned to retreat when armed warfare broke out between blacks and whites.

At a time when the Bug was the poster child for the love-and-peace movement, Manson was gazing into his cracked crystal ball and envisioning an entire army of Volkswagen-powered dune buggies leading him to victory. To Manson, the harmless Beetle was really a potent Beelzebub, inspiring him to name his garage of vehicle conversions the Devil's Dune Buggy Shop. While incarcerated, the crazed

Manson etched a swastika into his forehead in what one assumes to be a gesture of endearment to the late Nazi kingpin.

Serial murderer Ted Bundy was another nasty Bug devotee, whose cute light brown '68 with a canvas sunroof played a crucial role in his evil deeds. His first stalking ground was the beach in Seattle, Washington. Fitting his arm with a phony cast, Bundy tried to lure attractive women into his Beetle by innocently asking them for a hand with his sailboat. On separate occasions, three took the bait, riding with him in his Bug to where he claimed his boat was parked and then meeting their horrific deaths at his hands.

Later, after several murders in 1975, the homicidal sex fiend was apprehended by Utah police who pulled him over in his Beetle for traffic violations. Incriminating evidence linking him to the deaths was found in the Bug, but Bundy bolted town. After more murders, Bundy landed in Florida where, on the lam from the law, he made his fatal mistake: he stole a '72 orange Beetle, perhaps hoping for more sick Bug fun. Before he could act on his demented plans, he was busted for auto theft. After his arrest, his fugitive status as a serial murderer was discovered. Convicted in 1979, Bundy was executed in 1989.

In a twisted update on Bundy's 1968 tan Beetle, nearly twenty years after it was confiscated in Salt Lake City, a former sheriff's deputy there ran an ad in the *New York Times* offering to sell it for twenty-five thousand dollars. He claimed to have the original ownership papers with Bundy's signature. The ex-cop had paid nine hundred twenty-five dollars for it at a police auction in the late seventies and years later decided to cash in on Bundy's notoriety. Reportedly he received over three dozen offers.

### A Star in Its Own Right

The Volkswagen Beetle often brings its distinct personality to the screen. In many instances, a character drives one and without a word of dialogue you get the message: this person's attributes include trustworthiness and humility with a touch of non-conformity thrown in for good measure. Conversely, the Bug's spirit of innocence also works well to forebode diabolical action. Or plunk one down in a scene for color and it evokes a time (often the hippie era), a place (it's still the quintessential San Francisco car) or a sentiment (nostalgia for the bygone simple life). Like the fair prince disguised as an ugly frog, the Bug in film has the ability to confound expectations and offer poignant truths.

In an interview with *Entertainment Weekly*, GQ car columnist Owen Edwards said that the Bug's value to directors is that the car doesn't look like any other and its appeal to audiences is its eternal cuteness. His assessment? "It's *Gidget Goes to Detroit*."

The Vee Dub Bug hasn't had many starring roles in films other than the entertaining Walt Disney series of Herbie flicks. But it has frequently appeared in supporting and cameo roles. As a viewer, once you're aware of their prop value, especially to filmmakers who came of age in the sixties and seventies, you see Bugs everywhere. In the film *Sneakers*, Robert Redford drives a convertible with fellow high-tech expert Sidney Poitier as a passenger, while Richard Dreyfuss also tools around in a VW convertible in *The Big Fix*. In director Wes Craven's horror-genre sendup *Scream*, heroine Sidney Prescott (played by Neve Campbell) is pursued by a crazed masked killer when a friend comes to the rescue in a bright red-orange Bug. In *Star Trek IV: The Voyage Home*, Starship Enterprise commander James T. Kirk and crew come back in time to San Francisco, circa 1986, to save the whales. As they walk toward North Beach, a gray convertible inconspicuously passes by.

Although the Bug may always get the proverbial "walk on" (or in this case "drive on") role when it comes to Hollywood movies, it's also on the constant call-back list. Like a chameleon, it adapts to its part perfectly.

While the Bug was celebrated for being *the* cheap car to own, that didn't stop a rich man such as John Paul Getty II from driving one. And while his press relations corps

wouldn't verify the accuracy of the news story, it was rumored that the richest man in the world, Microsoft maestro Bill Gates, was wait-listed to buy a Beetle 2.0 in its early days on the marketplace. Even men in powerful political positions got behind the wheel of a Beetle if it was expedient. Case in point: German chancellor Willy Brandt made the politically correct decision to drive one during his tenure in office. In addition, car collectors such as Baseball Hall of Famer Reggie Jackson made certain that a Volkswagen got to hang out with his Corvettes, Camaros and Cobras.

The Bug also found favor with famous musicians. The late Beatle John Lennon owned one, as did rocker Eddie Van Halen. Singer-songwriter-actor Kris Kristofferson even found inspiration from a Volkswagen for a memorable line in his song, "Me and Bobby McGee." After earning his degree as a Rhodes Scholar at Oxford University in England in the seventies, he moved to Nashville, the country music capital, to try his hand at songwriting. He became one of the city's many Bugs, which is what songwriters were called there. While working on the tune that singer Janis Joplin would eventually put on the pop music map, Kristofferson struggled with the lyrics. He didn't come up with a final draft until he was driving his old Volkswagen to the airport in New Orleans during a rainstorm. The rhythm of the windshield wipers spurred the couplet, "Windshield wipers slapping time / I was holding Bobby's hand in mine."

Kristofferson worked as a janitor at the time to support his artistic habit. His choice of vehicle came out of necessity. Feisty folk-thrash singing star Ani DiFranco, who has recorded several albums on her own Righteous Babe label, was also forced to drive in the economy mode when she first started touring in the early nineties. The New York-based DiFranco played in California for the first time in January 1991. After her gigs, she needed to return home on a shoestring budget to play a date. She bought a '69 Bug in Los Angeles and hit the road, crossing the country in five days.

"It was a nightmare because the heater didn't work,"

recalls DiFranco, whose music is appropriately branded alternacoustic punk feminoid. "I kept having to pull over to sleep and it was so cold I felt like I was getting hypothermia." The Beetle got her safely to New York in time for the show.

Jazz cats were also hep to the Bug, man. Guitarist Al Di Meola, who launched his career in 1974 in pianist Chick Corea's fusion band and went on to become a successful solo artist, remembers borrowing his dad's yellow automatic Beetle to go to rehearsals with his buddies when he was a teenager. After one session, he blew the engine on his way home. "I thought my father was going to kill me," says Di Meola, who grew up in New Jersey. "But he was cool about it. He loved his Volkswagen. He was a guy who had other cars, but the Beetle was his favorite. His profession was carpentry. Instead of loading up a truck bed, he stuffed all his tools in the Bug's front trunk."

The Di Meola Beetle came to a tragic end. Parked in the garage, it started the family house on fire. Unbeknownst to the young, aspiring guitarist who was upstairs alone at the time practicing, the fire spread through the entire house. "The neighbors were trying to get to me, but I couldn't hear anything over the music," recalls Di Meola. "Soon the whole house was engulfed. Fortunately I got out with all my guitars and equipment. But the Volkswagen wasn't as lucky. I'll never forget its interior after the fire. All the leather melted like cheese on a pizza."

Another Beetle fan from the jazz scene is Cuban-born saxophonist Paquito D'Rivera, who not only has two Bugs parked at his New Jersey home, but also has a modest collection of Beetle toys. A founding member of the seminal Cuban jazz band Irakere and, after he defected to the U.S. in 1980, a member of Dizzy Gillespie's United Nation Orchestra, D'Rivera became enamored of the Volkswagen Sedan when his father test drove one in Havana. His dad almost bought the car, but soon thereafter Fidel Castro came to power and made such extravagant purchases impossible. "The Beetles survived the Castro revolution," says D'Rivera.

*Singer-actor Lyle Lovett, left, rented a black newby from Ken Kerzner, president of trendy Budget Rent-A-Car in Beverly Hills.*

*Previous spread: Roll over, Goofy. Herbie, the Love Bug and the Disney darling in 1969, wheeled his way to big-screen stardom. Above: Herbie commands a loyal audience. ©Disney Enterprises.*

"But most of them were owned by the big shots in the country. I'll never forget seeing the chief of the political police, Ramiro Valdes, driving past my house every day in one."

D'Rivera celebrated the birth of his son in 1988 by purchasing a green 1974 Beetle. Ten years later while visiting a friend who owns an ostrich farm in Pennsylvania Amish country, D'Rivera picked up a second Bug, an off-white '64 in mint condition. "My friend wanted to go to town to buy some ice cream," D'Rivera recalls. "I wasn't interested in the ice cream, but I decided to go anyway, which was lucky for me. Across the street from the ice cream shop was the car with a 'for sale' sign on it."

After buying the car and having it shipped to his house, D'Rivera was in for a surprise. When he took it for a drive, he thought the car was broken. But his mechanic assured him everything was fine, that the '64 simply didn't have the horsepower of his '74.

Why is D'Rivera, who named his music company

Green Bug Productions, so enthralled by the Beetle? "I'm captivated by the way it sounds. It's so rhythmic, especially the '64 which is really loud. But I also feel like I can relate to it, like it's alive. Maybe it's the eyes." He also finds the Beetle whimsically unique, comparing it to Dizzy Gillespie's singular upturned-bell trumpet. Plus, D'Rivera is a fan of the new Beetle, describing it in jazz lingo as "an American improvisation on a basic German theme."

The hip hop music community got a dose of Volkswagen fever in the mid nineties when white rap group the Beastie Boys made a fashion statement in their live shows. Rapper Mike D donned a circular VW medallion found on the front trunks of Bugs as a spoof on other hip hop artists wearing gold jewelry with logos of expensive cars such as BMW and Mercedes. The chintzy VW insignia Mike D wore lampooned rap styles at the time. The only problem was that Beastie Boys fans all over the country began prying the medallions off Bugs parked on the street.

In addition to musicians with Bugs on the brain, one record executive has a strong track record with Volkswagen. Don Rose, president and co-founder of the Salem, Massachusetts-headquartered Rykodisc Records, owns an award-winning Chinese red Karmann Ghia and a brand-spanking-new Beetle. When he was sixteen, Rose bought a VW bus, paid a guy thirty-five dollars to brush paint it with psychedelic-colored sunbursts, rainbows and mushrooms. He also bought a '65 Beetle convertible when he was twenty-two. It had a rusted-out Fred Flintstone-like floor with a piece of wood jammed in between the shift linkage tunnel and frame to keep the battery from falling out. In later years, he scooped up a primrose yellow '67 Beetle convertible with black interior originally owned by one of those proverbial little old ladies who only drove it to church on Sunday. Rose eventually sold it to make room in his garage, but bought a toy version as a memento.

*Woody Allen's affinity for the Beetle inspired him to work the model into the relationship act in two of his early films.*

It makes sense that Lyle Lovett, the maverick artist whose concerts teem with droll humor and self-deprecating wit, would have driven a homely little Beetle in a state where extra large rules. It's easy to imagine the tall Texan, with chiseled face and scarecrow physique, in a Bug. Just as the car's appeal upended criticism of its unsightly appearance, Lovett plays the role of quaint oddball with unflinching charm. He displayed this in his late eighties-early nineties tour during the rhythm and blues swing number "She's Hot To Go." After Lovett sang the lines, "She was ugly from the front / And I said this girl was so ugly…," the band skidded to a stop and back-up vocalist Francine Reed needled him on cue, "Well, you ugly too," before the group returned to its upbeat romp. In VW tradition, here was the unbecoming, yet immensely popular singer in the unattractive, yet wildly successful car—it's a perfect fit.

Lovett wasn't the only celeb smitten by the new Beetle. Larry Hagman, best known as bad guy J.R. Ewing on the night-time television soap opera *Dallas*, bought a new one,

as did *Wheel of Fortune* host Pat Sajak and pop group Fleetwood Mac founder Mick Fleetwood. Reminiscent of lofty basketball superstar Wilt Chamberlain appearing in a sixties Bug ad (tall man in a squat car), seven-foot-tall Los Angeles Lakers center Shaquille O'Neal took a new Beetle on a test drive, but didn't pull the trigger on the purchase, opting instead to pay cash for a Lexus.

On Oscar night in 1998, a fleet of new Beetles was unleashed on Hollywood with such luminaries as actors Robert Wagner and Jon Voight and comedian Jon Lovitz getting the opportunity to test out the new Volkswagen line. The car was an unqualified hit. While the old Bug had been a rarity in the upper echelons of celebrity society, the tables were turned with Beetle 2.0. It proved to be just as glamorous and attention-grabbing as the rich and famous drivers behind the wheel.

### Herbie with a Heart

Despite the ubiquity of the Beetle in films over the years, all roles pale in comparison to the car's marquee billing as Herbie. The adorable, feisty auto's stardom jumpstarted in 1969 with the fun-loving movie, *The Love Bug*, which spun off several sequels. Set in San Francisco, the sitcom/slapstick film co-stars love interests Dean Jones (washed-up race car driver Jim Douglas) and Michele Lee (car buff/mechanic Carole Bennett).

Herbie is introduced when Douglas walks into a European car dealership and asks, "What do you have in the way of cheap, honest transportation?" He lusts after the hot Euro models, but takes pity on the Bug. The canine-like Herbie follows Douglas home and eventually wins him over even though the Bug has a wild and crazy mind of its own. Its most appealing attribute to Jones is its fiery speed. "I think I can make something out of this sad bucket of bolts," he says, not realizing that Herbie is much more than a mere car. Herbie, like most Bugs in real life, has a personality. It gets angry (squirting motor oil on bad guy Peter Thorndyke every chance it gets), jealous (especially when his fickle owner buys a hot red Lambourgini), depressed (attempting suicide off the Golden Gate Bridge) and determined (winning the big race even after the villains have sabotaged him). He's also the matchmaker who chauffeurs the lovebirds.

The adventures of Herbie continued in three other Disney flicks, with such comedians as Don Knotts (*Herbie Goes to Monte Carlo*), Cloris Leachman and Harvey Korman (*Herbie Goes Bananas*) and Ken Barry, Stephanie Powers, Helen Hayes and Keenan Wynn (*Herbie Rides Again*). In the latter, Barry's character rejects the notion that the Bug is something special, telling Powers, "Let's stop kidding ourselves, shall we. This is just an ordinary little car, just like a million other ordinary, rather unattractive little cars." Insulted, the cute but cantankerous Herbie takes control and proves Barry wrong by romping through San Francisco on a hellsapoppin' ride. Of course, Herbie the hellion Love Bug becomes the hero at the end. He rounds up a Beetle battalion to wage war against the evil Alonzo Hawk (who insulted Herbie by saying, "A six-year-old kid could steal this one-cylinder hair dryer.") and leads the saccharine couple to the altar.

Walt Disney Productions has been responsible for some of America's best-loved characters, including Mickey Mouse and Donald Duck. But the creation of Herbie was a master stroke. *The Love Bug* not only tapped into the Volkswagen Beetle's beloved qualities but has also perpetuated its lovability for generations to come.

A VW plays a part in the pivotal fall-in-love scene from director Hal Ashby's seventies cult classic *Harold and Maude*. When the unlikely couple of young Harold, a macabre sort who feigns suicide to get his socialite mother's goat, and octogenarian Maude, an eccentric free spirit whose philosophy is "try something new each day," meet, they are standing in front of a powder-blue Beetle. Both have been attending a funeral, a bizarre pastime they share.

In front of the church after the mass, Harold and Maude converse for the first time, then she takes her leave, saying with a twinkle in her eye, "We shall have to meet again." Quirky and non-conformist to the nth degree, Maude climbs behind the wheel of the Bug, pulls a wide U-turn over the curb and with squealing tires speeds off. The priest who had been officiating the service runs out into the street yelling, "That woman, she took my car." In subsequent scenes, Maude drives other cars, including an Oldsmobile and a Mustang that she has stolen on a whim. But the Bug is a Maude auto, a car that like her canary-freeing character (one of her great lines is "How the world dearly loves a cage") defies expectations and the status quo.

### Woody and the Bug

It's the year 2073 and thirty-five-year-old Greenwich Village resident Miles Monroe is scrambling to escape from having his brain "electronically simplified" by the Security Police in a clampdown society. Two hundred years earlier Miles had entered a hospital for routine treatment of a minor peptic ulcer. Instead he was cryogenically preserved for posterity. Pursued by the bungling Keystone Cops-like Security Police, Miles and the beautiful poet Luna find themselves holed up in a cave pondering their next move when he spots a relic from the past: a two-hundred-year-old Volkswagen Beetle. He climbs in behind the wheel of the now ancient auto and sure enough the engine turns right over. "Wow, they really built these things, didn't they," Miles says as he and Luna take off through the countryside in their dust-encrusted, yet reliable getaway vehicle. Soon Miles decides to destroy evidence of their escape and enlists Luna to push the Bug over a cliff into a stream. In one of the most tragic Beetle scenes ever filmed, the car plunges to its death.

The movie is Woody Allen's 1973 sci-fi comedy *Sleeper* and the protagonists are played by Allen and Diane Keaton. While it only plays a small role in the flick, the Bug makes its presence indelibly felt.

"Can we order one with bat fins?"

# Rent-a-Bug

$U$nless you're vacationing in Mexico where Bugs continue to be spawned in the Volkswagen factory, chances are slim to nil that you'll be able to rent an old-styled Volkswagen Beetle. However, there are a couple of rental agencies in the Los Angeles area where you might be able to score one for a spell.

### Rent-A-Wreck

This West Los Angeles rental company, which serves a mostly affluent and middle-class clientele looking for hip vintage cars to tool around in, used to have over a hundred Bugs for the taking. But its stock has dwindled to fifteen—some well-worn and dented—that are primarily rented for use in movies, music videos and commercials. Ranging in model years from the late sixties to mid seventies, these cars generally show up onscreen as props. The agency has even been known to repaint Bugs to meet the requests of a film's art director. While Rent-A-Wreck says it doesn't lease its Beetles to run-of-the-mill customers, tote a camera along with you. You might be able to convince the guys at the lot that you're serious about making a film of some sort and be able to grab one for a day.

### Bug City

While owner Mark Fogel ran a car rental agency for years at his present location on South La Cienega Boulevard in Los Angeles, he changed the name of the lot to Bug City in 1998 to publicize the fact that he rents Volkswagen Beetles. He has several classic convertibles from the late seventies. Yet he admits that dealing in older cars that are more prone to breakdowns poses a major problem. His solution? Import brand new Beetles made in Mexico, bring them up to snuff to comply with EPA auto standards and then rent those little Buggies. His publicly-traded Nostalgia Motor Car Corporation also plans to reintroduce the old-styled Bug back into the American car sales market.

### Budget Rent-A-Car of Beverly Hills

Independent of the nationwide Budget car rental company, Budget of Beverly Hills prides itself in being the first on the block to stock the hottest cars on the market. Rather than supply three or four new car models, BBH has a fifteen hundred-car fleet comprising over eight hundred models, including such elite cars as BMWs, Volvos, Mercedes and Vipers as well as top of the line American models. It's no surprise that Budget rents to Hollywood celebrities and politicians. It's also no surprise that BBH was the first car rental company to deal in new Beetles. While president Ken Kerzner cites client confidentiality for not naming names of his clientele, he does note that singer-actor Lyle Lovett was the first celeb to rent one. When they first appeared, new Beetles rented for between seventy-nine and ninety-nine dollars per day.

Woody Allen's affinity for the Beetle inspired him to work the model into the relationship act in two of his other early films. In 1972's *Play It Again, Sam*, movie buff Alan (played by Allen) gets dumped by his wife Nancy (Susan Anspach) who splits in an off-white, banged up Bug. Later, Allen falls for Diane Keaton's character who's married to his best friend. With the help of a fantasy Humphrey Bogart, he wins over her affection, although it's not easy. At one point, he argues with the meddling ghost Bogie, echoing the endearing qualities of a Beetle, "I'm short and ugly enough to succeed on my own."

A few years later in *Annie Hall*, another Allen-Keaton comedy, Woody plays the Bug card again, this time using a gold convertible to serve as the vehicle in which their romance is sparked. La-de-da Annie, played by Keaton, offers Alvie Singer, Allen's character, a ride home. After a harrowing drive through New York City streets, Singer gets out of the Bug and says, "You're the worst driver I've ever seen in my life." But that doesn't stop him from hopping in the Beetle a couple of days later to go with her to the Hamptons. After *Annie Hall*, the Bug dropped off Allen's map.

### The Bug's Darker Side

In movies, the VW has also been used as an unassuming car that takes its unsuspecting passengers into the doomed zone. Case in point: *The Shining*, Stanley Kubrick's brilliant, relentless 1980 horror film starring Jack Nicholson and Shelley Duvall. The thriller, based on the Stephen King book, begins innocently enough with Nicholson's character Jack Torrance driving a benign-looking yellow Volkswagen Beetle up a meandering twenty-five-mile road called the Sidewinder to the secluded Overlook Hotel.

Jack decides to take the job as the hotel's winter caretaker, which marks the beginning of his family's roller coaster ride into hell. Another Bug surfaces, this time a red one crushed under a jack-knifed big rig during a storm. It's a harbinger of more chilling deeds to come.

The Bug has also offered a number of nightmare drives to characters in the *Friday the 13th* films. Those flicks feature the creepy character Jason Voorhees who has a penchant for violently doing in teenagers. In a whimsical essay in the *Seattle Times*, C. Ray Hall detailed thirteen lessons to be had from the popular horror series. One pointer is that anyone driving a Bug is doomed.

The ultimate sinister Beetle is the spiky one that leads an entire squad of growling autos that take revenge on an Australian town's citizens in *The Cars That Ate Paris*, noted director Peter Weir's debut film released in 1974. The economy of Paris, an isolated countryside village in Austrailia, is driven by car salvaging operations generated by horrendous crashes that take place in the vicinity. The corrupt mayor and city council are behind the insidious accidents. The despicable status quo they uphold is eventually upended by the demolition derby-like mutant cars pieced together with spare parts. They are vicious machines that attack the town, destroying it with a vengeance. The scariest of the cars is the killer Beetle, which ominously moves through the dark and punctures its victims with its huge thorns.

Several years and films later, Weir uses a Volkswagen Bug again, this time as a key image in 1998's *The Truman Show*. The car helps to rescue the Jim Carrey character Truman Burbank whose entire life, unbeknownst to him, has been captured on camera in a long-running television series. He finally begins to suspect there's more to life than his idyllic island home of Seahaven while sitting in his car one day. Looking in his rear-view mirror, he discovers that the world surrounding him is operating on a tape loop system. He pulls his wife into the car and predicts that in the next moment she'll see a lady riding a red bike, a man walking by with flowers and a yellow Volkswagen Beetle with a dented fender driving through. The Bug appears again and liberates him. "There's the dented Beetle, Yes!" exclaims Truman, who from then on rebels against the mold the show creator has designed for him. Another victory for the Bug.

The first
Beetle sold in the
U.S. cost eight hundred
dollars. The year
was 1949.

## beetle basics
# BugRoots

The first thing you observe when you arrive by train in Wolfsburg, Germany, is the massive Volkswagen factory on the north bank of Mittelland Canal. There's the universally recognizable blue and white VW emblem on the side of a huge brick building, which has four smokestacks that resemble Beetle exhaust pipes. That's only a small part of the Volkswagenwerk operation, which is the world's largest auto factory. The buildings cover close to four hundred acres. In 1998, it employed sixty thousand workers who produced over two hundred thousand cars that year, sadly none of them Beetles.

The Volkswagen factory has come a long way since 1938 when ground was broken in a swampy field not far from the small village of Fallersleben and Wolfsburg Castle. It barely survived World War II, struggled through the lean post-war years and scrambled for respectability in the days when large and luxurious cars were in demand.

Wolfsburg, one of the most modern cities in Germany, boasts a vibrant city center, new art and theater buildings and well-designed pedestrian and bicycle paths. Yet, with such a high percentage of its populace employed by Volkswagen, it is in many ways an old-fashioned company town. But for Bug fans, Wolfsburg is the birthplace, the natural habitat in which the humble People's Car grew up and went on to conquer the world. Even though the last Bug came off the assembly line of the mother factory in 1974, pilgrims continue to journey to Wolfsburg to pay their respects.

It's one of the many Bug ironies that a car so aligned with the left-wing counterculture of America in the sixties would have such a shadowy past. By most accounts, the Volkswagen history begins with Ferdinand Porsche, the genius car designer who imagined the Beetle into being in the early thirties, and Adolph Hitler, who exercised his political might to fund the infrastructure necessary for production of the car. The Volkswagen, which literally means "People's Car" in German, was Hitler's offspring. However, the seed was planted many years earlier not by a German, but an American: Henry Ford, who

## POSTWAR VOLKSWAGENWERK

Following World War II, the Volkswagen factory, under the authority of the British occupation forces, was up for grabs. In 1945, a British commission predicted the bombed-out plant would soon collapse and recommended against investment in the facility by England's auto industry. Twice more in 1946, the factory was offered to, and turned down by, the British. The following year the Australian Reparations Commission likewise rejected an offer to run Volkswagenwerk. Even after Heinz Nordoff took over control of the factory as its general manager, the British tried one last time in 1948 to pawn off the plant, this time to American auto giant Ford Motor Company, which already had substantial investments in Germany. The asking price? Free. Ernest Beech, Ford's chairman of the board, told Henry Ford II the plant wasn't "worth a damn" and declined the offer.

The only interested post-war party was the Soviet Union. In 1948 it requested that the border line demarcating East Germany (in the Soviet sphere of influence) from West Germany (soon to be independently run by its own central government) be redrawn five miles further west so Wolfsburg and Volkswagenwerk could be under its control. The Soviet offer to run the factory was refused.

*In 1937 a Beetle prototype spun around a corner on a test drive in Germany.*

pioneered mass-produced automobiles via the assembly line approach. He built the first true car of the common folk, the Model T.

Porsche revered Ford for his auto innovations. In addition, Hitler held the mighty U.S. capitalist in high esteem for a variety of other less savory reasons. During the twenties, Ford's name was synonymous with the car industry, but he was also closely linked to a heinous anti-Semitic conspiracy theory. Hitler was impressed by Ford's brilliance in business matters, but, more than likely, it was a shared sympathetic social doctrine that led the budding tyrant in 1922 to hang a large photo of the car maker in his political party headquarters.

Ford's Model T, also known as the flivver, Lizzie and Tin Lizzie, was produced from 1908 to 1927. Without changing its basic design, the car eventually reached sales figures of over fifteen million. (Volkswagen later adopted a similar keep-the-same-design strategy with the Beetle, which resulted in the modest Bug wresting the sales record from Ford.) The Model T made Ford rich and powerful. In 1918, he purchased the *Dearborn Independent* newspaper, which he distributed through his car dealers. Ford called the editorial shots, authorizing all the news and opinions that appeared in the paper. It wasn't long before his bigotry became as well known as his car.

In 1920, the *Independent* launched a twenty-one-month assault on Jews with a series of anti-Semitic articles called "The International Jew: The World's Problem." The basic thesis centered on accusations that the international Jewish banking community was exerting its influence to instigate wars and destroy Christian civilization. It was a conspiracy theory of half-baked truths and full-fledged lies. Shortly after the articles appeared in the newspaper, they were collected into a book, *The International Jew*, with authorship assigned to Henry Ford. It became a best seller in Germany, where it fueled widespread anti-Semitic sentiments.

German publishers translated it into several languages

and disseminated it worldwide. In essence, Ford's book, which espoused an anti-Jewish social, economic and political order, fanned the flames of the Nazi agenda, which subscribed to the same anti-Semitic philosophy. Hitler celebrated Ford in his book *Mein Kampf*, labeling him the greatest American in history.

In 1924, the *Independent* published a second series of Jew-baiting articles called the "Jewish Exploitation of Farmer Organizations." Three years later under pressure of lawsuits, Ford apologized publicly, but by then the damage had been done. Sensing that Ford was a kindred spirit, Hitler solicited him via an emissary for donations to the Nazi cause. (It was never proved that Ford made contributions.)

Yet the car maker continued to do business with the Nazi regime throughout the thirties. Ford had an assembly plant in Cologne and opened a new factory in Berlin as late as 1939 when Germany already was revving up its war machine. In 1938, Ford was presented with Hitler's Supreme Order of the German Eagle, the highest honor the Third Reich bestowed on non-Germans, in recognition of his trailblazing endeavors in automobile mass production.

By then, recognizing the true intentions of the Nazis and his own culpability in their gaining a stronghold in Germany, Ford accepted the award in the name of the German people, not the Third Reich. He also urged America to open its doors to the immigration of Jewish refugees fleeing Germany. A short time later, the Nazis used both Ford plants to churn out military vehicles. By then Hitler's own auto factory, built to produce Volkswagens, had also been retooled to manufacture war machines.

The Volkswagen was essentially born in 1935 when Porsche, employed by Hitler, developed three prototypes in his Stuttgart shop. An auto enthusiast even though he never learned to drive, Hitler was committed to making good on his promise to the German people to build an affordable "People's Car." He found sympathetic ears with Porsche, who had already been working on a cheap but efficient

*Above top: Ferdinand Porsche dreamed the Bug into being in the thirties. Above: The Bug overtook the Model T in sales in February 1972. Opposite: Early Bug prototypes awaited trial runs in a German village.*

## WOLFSBURG: THE CITY THE BEETLE BUILT

1938—Ground is broken for the Volkswagen factory near the small Lower Saxony region village of Fallersleben, best known for August Heinrich Hoffmann, the poet who composed the German national anthem. Land was requisitioned by the government from reluctant property owners in the area, including Count Werner von der Schulenburg, who owned the medieval Wolfsburg Castle. The settlement that grew up around the car factory was known as Town of the KdF-Wagens.

1945—The town council officially decrees the name Wolfsburg, making it one of Germany's newest cities. Its crest (a wolf, a two-towered castle and the waters of Mittelland Canal) appear on the front hood of early Beetles.

1955—The millionth Volkswagen rolls off the factory assembly line as Wolfsburg holds a groundbreaking ceremony for its new town hall, which would be completed in 1958.

1972—Wolfsburg incorporates twenty boroughs, including Fallersleben, and increases its population to 131,000.

1982—Well-known as the auto capital of Germany, Wolfsburg gets its link to the autobahn, the high-speed German superhighway.

## WHO OWNS VOLKSWAGEN?

Since its founding, Volkswagen has undergone a number of ownership changes:

Pre-World War II—In 1937, the Nazis formed the Volkswagen Development Company for the sole purpose of implementing Adolph Hitler's dream of building the "People's Car." Its management team included designer Ferdinand Porsche and German Labor Front official Dr. Bodo Lafferentz. The German Labor Front, which sponsored the KdF organization, financed Volkswagen.

During World War II—The Third Reich operated and controlled Volkswagenwerk, which was converted into a military operation.

Post-World War II—Shortly after the defeat of Germany, the Allied Military Government oversaw the operations of Volkswagen. In 1949, the West German government took over the trusteeship of the company, delegating partial control to the region of Lower Saxony. In 1961, Volkswagenwerk AG went public, with sixty percent of the company offered to stockholders.

compact car as early as 1931 when the world depression was deepening, the Weimar Republic was close to collapse and the German auto industry was nearly bankrupt. It was his "Project 12 - The Small Car" design that eventually evolved into the air-cooled, four-cylinder, rear-engine Bug.

After Hitler assumed power in Germany, he proclaimed at the 1933 Berlin Motor Show that the country would soon build a small car to "motorize the people." Hitler met with Porsche and outlined his Volks-list of requirements: cruising speed of sixty mph, low fuel consumption, air-cooled engine in the rear, cheap cost and roomy enough to carry four adults. Most likely, Hitler had world conquest on his mind as he sketched out the essentials. A vehicle not requiring a radiator could survive hot temperatures (read: the deserts of northern Africa) as well as extreme frigid conditions (read: Russia). With an air-cooled system, there would be no radiator water to overheat or freeze. Also with the engine in the rear, good traction would be guaranteed on less-than-ideal roadways.

In 1937, the dictator ordered the construction of a new factory in the Lower Saxony district of Germany (later to become the city of Wolfsburg) for the manufacture of the "People's Car." In May 1938, shortly after he annexed Austria, Hitler attended the groundbreaking ceremony and laid the cornerstone of the Volkswagen factory. Little did he realize then that not a single car would be produced for the people during his lifetime.

Boasting that he would outdo Ford at his own game, Hitler was firm in his commitment to build the car, which was sponsored by the Nazi propaganda/leisure time organization *Kraft durch Freude* (KdF), or "Strength-through-Joy." In August 1938, the KdF announced how a German citizen could purchase the KdF-Wagen: employees would participate in an innovative five-mark-per-month installment plan. While the layaway funds would not draw interest (making it similar to a modern-day, bank-sponsored Christmas club), a car was promised in a little over four years.

*Opposite: Back to the drawing board: early VW3G prototypes with louvered engine lids were destroyed, circa 1942. Above: Hitler approved of the Volkswagen's spacious back seat. Left: For five marks a week, German citizens could buy a Volkswagen (called the KdF-Wagen). Payment stamps were collected in these booklets.*

However, Hitler's wartime exploits eclipsed the production of the car for civilian use; and the Volkswagen plant was blemished by another Third Reich dictate: slave labor. Seventy percent of the factory workers were prisoners from Nazi-occupied countries such as Poland, France and the Netherlands. Many of the coerced laborers were transferred to Volkswagen headquarters from concentration camps. (Historians estimate that under the Hitler regime more than seven million people were forced to work for several German companies, including automakers BMW, Daimler-Benz and Audi as well as the electronics company Siemens and in the Krupp steel mills.)

At the Volkswagen site, the slave laborers worked grueling twelve-hour days under the constant supervision of Nazi guards. Discipline was harsh and workers survived on near-starvation diets. In an Associated Press news story by Chelsea J. Carter, one victim, who as a teenager was taken from Auschwitz to work at Volkswagen, was quoted as saying that while the concentration camp was hell, the factory "was the skirt of the hell."

(In 1998, a federal class-action lawsuit was filed in New York on behalf of the surviving slave laborers of the Nazi era. The suit demanded compensation for their work. While Volkswagen AG denied any legal responsibility for what took place at the Nazi-run facility during the war, the company created a twelve million dollar compensation fund, acknowledging a "moral responsibility" to the people who were enslaved. By doing so, the automaker's executives also hoped to deflect a barrage of bad publicity.)

Since the factory manufactured thousands of military vehicles based on the Volkswagen design, it became a war target. On April 8, 1944, it was bombed for the first time by the Allied air forces. After several other raids, it was estimated that as much as sixty percent of the factory was destroyed.

After the war, the British became overseers of the sector of Germany where the factory was located. Even though

Not a single Volkswagen was produced for the "people" during Hitler's lifetime.

## PRIMER ON THE KdF-WAGEN

The Volkswagen Beetle was first manifested as the Nazi-funded *Kraft durch Freude* (Strength-through-Joy) car. Called the KdF-Wagen, it was to be Adolph Hitler's gift to the masses. He boasted that ten million *Volksautos* would be manufactured for the "chosen" populace.

On August 1, 1938, the KdF organization (established by the Nazi-led, pro-employer German Labor Front) announced its layaway policy.

Between 1938 and 1945, 336,668 German workers purchased KdF-Wagen savings stamps at local KdF offices, depositing a total of sixty-seven million dollars. Not one car was delivered to KdF-Wagen savers.

Although it was assumed that Hitler used the cash to bankroll his military endeavors, all funds were deposited in the Bank of German Labor in Berlin. After the war, the Russian occupation force seized the money.

On May 5, 1949, KdF-Wagen savers filed a lawsuit against the newly-installed West German government, which assumed the debts of the Third Reich. In 1961, after years of legal struggles, a settlement was worked out: KdF-Wagen savers would either receive one hundred marks in cash or a six-hundred-mark credit toward the purchase of a new Volkswagen. Half the eighty-seven thousand claimants bought Beetles.

*Bug parade: New Volkswagens made their debut in Berlin in 1939. The cars were driven only by high-ranking government officials.*

## BEETLE MILESTONES

1946—In March, the one thousandth Beetle is built at Volkswagenwerk in Wolfsburg, Germany.

1949—In May, the ten thousandth postwar VW is produced in Wolfsburg. The plant celebrates with a meal consisting of noodles and goulash. The Swiss unexpectedly send a birthday cake made with flour, and another postwar luxury, real coffee.

1949—The first Beetle is imported into the United States.

1967—The first Beetle is produced in VW's Puebla, Mexico, factory.

1968—423,000 Bugs are sold in the U.S., making this the car's peak sales year.

1972—In February, the 15,007,034th Beetle rolls off the assembly line in Wolfsburg, thus surpassing the record held by the Ford Model T and establishing the Bug as the all-time auto champion.

1974—The last Beetle is produced at the mother factory in Wolfsburg.

1978—The last Beetle is built at the factory in Emden, Germany.

1979—The last Beetle (a convertible) is sold in the U.S.

1998—Still built in Puebla, Mexico, the original Beetle is recognized by *The Guiness Book of World Records* as the model with the longest production run: 21,240,657. The new Beetle, also built in Puebla, is introduced in America.

the building was so badly damaged it was designated for dismantling, British army officer Major Ivan Hirst was placed in charge and safeguarded the facility. He set up a repair shop for Allied vehicles and made plans for building new cars. One KdF-Wagen built before the war was spray-painted green and so impressed British military authorities that Hirst was authorized to supervise the production of the Volkswagens with a work force of Germans and war refugees. By the end of 1945 the factory—the only source of work in the war-impoverished area—produced nearly two thousand cars. It's another Bug irony that the forces responsible for defeating Hitler actualized one of his pet projects. In October 1946 starving workers in a factory still filled with rubble rolled the ten thousandth Volkswagen off the assembly line.

*Opposite: Happy Birthday, Adolph. Ferdinand Porsche, in suit, presented the Führer with one of twelve VW convertibles made in 1939. Above: The first KdF-Wagens made at the new factory in 1941 featured special dimmed headlights for wartime.*

When the British exhausted attempts to find takers for the factory, they placed Volkswagenwerk in the command of German automobile industrialist Heinz Nordhoff. The year was 1948. The new factory manager wasted no time. By 1949 when the British officially turned over ownership to authorities of the newly created West Germany, Nordhoff was well on his way to pumping up the production of the Volkswagen Beetle.

Volkswagen took advantage of the recovering economy of the post-war period and, while stubbornly refusing to compromise the basic design of the model, manufactured thousands of the cars. Six years, a few trifling modifications (including the replacement of the split rear window with a single-paned one) and a million Volkswagens later, the company was well on its way to becoming the first foreign auto company to seriously challenge the American car industry. Nordoff, who continued at the helm of VW operations until his death in 1968, achieved what became known as the "Volkswagen miracle."

A final irony: The Little Car That Could eventually made Volkswagen one of the most successful automobile companies in the world. Over the years, there have been plenty of jokes contrasting the lowly, diminutive Beetle with the elite, luxurious Rolls-Royce. Place the two side-by-side—the blue-collar commoner with the status symbol of the rich and famous—and you get an automatic comic image. But Volkswagen got the last laugh. In 1998, the House That Beetle Built bought Rolls-Royce Motor Company from Vickers P.L.C. As a part of the deal, Volkswagen also acquired the rights to produce the Bentley, another upscale, handmade British car.

It proved to be a convoluted deal full of merger intrigue spurred by Volkswagen outbidding BMW, another German car giant. Because of complicated legal rights over the use of the name Rolls-Royce, Volkswagen was forced to negotiate an agreement with BMW, which had a long-standing business relationship with Rolls. The upshot: Volkswagen acquired the rights to both Rolls-Royce and Bentley until January 1, 2003, when Rolls would become BMW's property.

**4**

A cigarette lighter was standard equipment on the Beetle for the first time in 1979, the last year the Bug was sold in America.

# clubs & rituals
# BugFest

In the early fifties when there were only a handful of Volkswagen Beetles on American roadways, drivers waved and honked their horns at each other. It was a way of expressing camaraderie at a time when the more popular vehicles were wide-bodied, finned and pumped up with V-8 power. However, as the Bug gained popularity, it increasingly became impractical for fellow Vee Dub owners to acknowledge each other—you'd be honking and waving all day. So, there had to be an alternative to keep the *esprit de corps* alive. The solution came in the mid fifties when VW clubs were born. Club meetings were not only great opportunities for people to share their fondness for the car, but they were also a means by which to break bread—and swap parts—with other Bug owners.

Within a short time, dozens of VW clubs spread across the country and around the world. There are several chapters of the Volkswagen Club of America (which doesn't discriminate against models, including the latest Volkswagen fleet) as well as the Vintage Volkswagen Club of America (perhaps the largest organization). In Seattle, there's the Volkswagen Split Window Club of America dedicated to people specifically interested in pre-1953 Volkswagens with the double-paned rear window. In Nevada, a group of Volkswagen enthusiasts banded together as the Bad Influence VW Club. In Pennsylvania, there's the Bug Pack of Philadelphia and in Thorndale the VW Ego Club. Wiley's Thunderbugs meets in Marion, North Carolina. Other regional VW societies in the U.S. include the Granite State Vee-Dub Club in South Hampton, New Hampshire; the Good Times VW Club in Eugene, Oregon; the River City Air-Coolers in Collierville, Tennessee; Bugnuts VW Club of West Texas in Colorado City, Texas; Lightning Bugs in Kennewick, Washington; Wolfsburg's Wickedest in Modesto, California; and the B.Y.O.B. Air-Cooled VW Club in Milwaukee, Wisconsin.

Clubs hold meetings for members to gab about their Bugs. They sponsor events such as swap meets, weekend drives and even pilgrimages to the birthplace of the Beetle in Wolfsburg, Germany. Members offer each other advice on fix-it problems, share slides from their latest Bug adventures and even stage one-upmanship contests, engaging in trivia challenges such as what differentiates a fifties Beetle from one built in the mid sixties.

In the heart of high-tech Silicon Valley, California, a large group of Bug lovers convene to praise the epitome of automotive low-tech: Volkswagens, especially the classic pre-seventies varieties. Upwards of a hundred Vee Dub devotees from around the San Francisco Bay Area cram into a meeting room at Harry's Hofbrau in Mountain View, not far from San Jose, to attend the monthly gathering of the Golden Gate chapter of the Vintage Volkswagen Club of America. They arrive via the nearby freeway and park their bijoux in the hofbrau lot next to nondescript Hondas and Chevrolets owned by the establishment's other diners.

Soon after the new Beetle was introduced, the vintage Beetle owners congregated to share their opinions on it as well as attend to other club matters. The meeting was presided over by Rick Spohn, an IBM employee and VW collector who owns five Bugs: a '52 convertible, a '53 with a sunroof, a '56 convertible, a '56 sedan and a '66 convertible.

Even before the meeting officially began, several members were hunkered down in booths, telling stories of field trips to swap meets. There was a twentysomething guy with a couple of earrings, a couple other young men with long hair and grease-stained hands, a few married couples, several salty-dog VW owners and a scattering of women ranging in age from late teens to sixty plus. One booth of guys poured over the latest copy of *VW Trends* magazine while in another booth three members prepared a carousel of slides snapped on their recent trip to Germany to attend a Volkswagen rally.

A few minutes after eight, Spohn brought the meeting to order, standing in front of a club banner with the handsome image of a vintage Bug superimposed over a

*Give me a V, give me a W: hippie wanna-bes banded together to form the Volkswagen Club at Nottingham High School in Syracuse, New York, in 1971.*

bridge. He gently reminded people that treasurer Lydia Avak (who owns a '59 Bug she bought as new in Wolfsburg) was present to collect overdue membership fees (ten bucks a year). Then Spohn got down to business, by reminding people of the upcoming biannual VW bash in Solvang in Central California. He urged members to make plans quickly because the block of rooms reserved at a local hotel was bound to book up. It was to be the fifth such event in Solvang since the VW jamboree started there in 1990.

Next came a report from a few people who accompanied club historian Lois Grace on her VW caravan to the beach.

Spohn asked how it went. "It was fun and relaxing even though it was a little foggy," replied one participant. Did you all jump in the ocean? "Absolutely." How many cars went? "Twelve," one member reported, then added, "But my car died on the way. You should have seen it. Ten of us trying to rebuild the carburetor on the side of the highway."

A moment later a new member stood up and introduced himself. "I had a Volkswagen in high school but I got rid of it," said Scott Leatherman. "I recently found myself with an extra thousand dollars in my back pocket and decided to invest it in an old VW. I just bought a '58 Bug that I'm going to fix up with original stock." He was greeted with applause.

*Bug classics: a classic split window, left; Bob Shaill's 1952 Stoll Coupe, above.*

64

After a verbal classified of parts, accessories and cars for sale, the slides were projected on the wall. There were shots of an unrestored '46 Beetle, a shop with a wall of VW hubcaps and several antique Bugs driving to the rally in a town square. "We were excited," the attendees said. "There were about fifty splits and fifty ovals in one place." Translation: fifty cars with early-model split rear windows and fifty with the small, oval-shaped rear windows. A couple members discussed manufacture years, noting minute differences in a car's appearance invisible to the untrained eye. Then there were several slides of Beetle-based Nazi military vehicles, including the

amphibious *Schwimwagen*.

After the official meeting, people hung out in the parking lot to discuss the new Beetle, as Jan Peters, the founder of the chapter, gave rides in his silver, diesel-powered newby, showing off its speed, quickness and maneuverability. He's a Volkswagenphile, whose passion for the brand is infectious and knowledge of the cars encyclopedic. He's proud of the camaraderie he helped to instill. "You know, it's more than a club," he said in an emotional voice. "It's family."

Beetles survive in greater numbers on the West Coast because they find the temperate climate more to their liking. In mild conditions they don't have to deal with foul weather, which dramatically

*Lois Grace's 1958 convertible, left; Yunus Peer's '67 sedan, above.*

# Beetle Meets Ford

"I love my little Bug," says Linda Kowalski of her '65 Fontana Beige Bug. "It's like having a puppy. It's small and cute. And kids love running over to it and petting it. The kids like my Model A Ford coupe too. They jump up and down on its running board."

Ford meets the Beetle in Kowalski's Redwood City, California, garage. Joining her Bug are three Model A's: a '29 Speedster and two coupes, a '30 and a '31.

Kowalski's club schedule is packed. In addition to being a member of the Golden Gate chapter of the Vintage Volkswagen Club of America, she holds a membership in the Model A Ford Club of America and goes to meetings of two local chapters, Santa Clara and the El Camino A's in San Mateo. "I dated a fellow for four years who was really into old cars," she explains. "When I gave him up, it didn't make any sense giving up on the cars. I enjoy having the old Model A's as my second cars."

Kowalski has a rich Beetle history. Her father bought her a '57 when she was old enough to drive. "But he was a screamer when I was trying to learn," she explains. "I had no experience with a stick on the floor, so he gave up trying to teach me." Dad sold that car and bought her a clunky Ford station wagon. A few years later when she went to school, she got a brand new '59 Bug and kept the car when she got married. When the couple moved to Minnesota, they towed the Bug behind a Plymouth station wagon and spun around the countryside with it, raising the ire of the rural locals who still referred to it as Hitler's car.

They lived so far in the country, they had to have parts shipped to them via Greyhound bus when the engine went bad. After Kowalski and her husband divorced, she returned to California, sold the car, which never ran well after the engine repairs, and went without a Beetle until the mid eighties. When she decided to return to the Bug fold, instead of a newer model, Kowalski opted for the '65.

The car has proved to be a good companion to the Model A's. "A six-volt is a six-volt," she says referring to both makes requiring six-volt batteries. "I could switch the Bug and the Model A's to twelve-volt systems, but I like those six-volt cars. Of course, my friends kid me that when I drive I need to have someone run ahead with a lantern. It's true. The lights are dim."

lessens their life spans, and salt-crusted winter highways, which quickly corrode their otherwise impenetrable shells. So it comes as no surprise that West Coast clubs proliferated during the Beetle's heydays. According to a 1972 article in the magazine *Hot VWs*, by the mid sixties there were over a hundred associations in California alone.

However, Bugs still make rare appearances throughout the rest of the country, especially during the summer months when they come out from their garage cocoons. And wherever Beetles traipse, clubs thrive. It can be argued that in the Midwest and on the East Coast where the Bug is an endangered species, bonds among owners are even stronger than their counterparts on the West Coast, where Beetle specimens are still plentiful.

"It's sad that Beetles are nearly nonexistent on roads here," says Bill Cooney, who lives in Carlisle, Massachusetts, outside of Boston. "They used to be so ubiquitous. Now they're the exception."

Cooney owns one of those automotive rarities, a blue '55 Bug with a sunroof that he bought in 1985, coincidentally, from Jan Peters of the Golden Gate chapter of the Vintage Volkswagen Club. Cooney knew him through the club network. Peters advertised the car in the national club newsletter. Since he was the chapter president at the time, Cooney trusted him. "It was a calculated risk, but I bought the car on faith," explains Cooney. "I only saw photos of it. I had it delivered by car carrier. It was actually in better condition than I expected it to be. It was totally rust-free and was all original."

Cooney calls the car his "perpetual project." He drives it often, but avoids unfavorable weather, even rainy days. He tucks it away for a winter-early spring hibernation, elevating it off his garage floor with jack stands. In 1998, Cooney even took the car to Nantucket Island to drive it in the Daffodil Parade of antique cars. There were one hundred fifty cars in the parade and his was the only Bug. All

weekend, people approached him with their VW tales.

Back in California, new clubs continue to crop up. Roscoe Walker of Burlingame, an upscale bedroom community south of San Francisco, established his "totally underground" Old Volks in 1992. Why? Because he and his young Beetle-minded friends started recognizing people waving at them when they drove their vintage Volkswagens around town.

Walker got his first Beetle when he was sixteen and owned twenty-four by the time he turned twenty-four. He unearths them in people's backyards, buys them, fixes them up and then gives his friends good deals. He also encourages Bugdom fraternity by staging modest Bug fests.

In the summer of 1998, Walker staged one of his first Old Volks meets. It featured three dozen old Bugs—including a few souped-up racers you wouldn't want to mess with on the freeway—parked in the lot of an antique store in Burlingame. He put the word out at the Vintage Volkswagen meeting and to his Bug friends around the state. A contingent of cars arrived from as far away as Modesto in the Central Valley to participate. In addition to the cars on display, the event attracted a couple dozen other Bugs, which were parked along the street. It was a rare free show with hourly raffles. Prizes included a ten-pack of valve cover gaskets, t-shirts and distributor covers—stocking stuffers highly valued by the crowd.

Dressed in sunglasses, shorts and an old white Old Volks T-shirt, Walker clearly enjoyed himself. He had a good turnout. It was a sunny summer day and the music—a trip-hop blend of electronica—blared from the loudspeakers of a VW van. Vee Dub fans salivated over the classic cars, including a bright cherry red '56 convertible with a luggage rack, a '62 powder blue convertible, a '50 green sedan with a split rear window and several mid fifties cars with oval-shaped rear windows. Even though people of all ages attended, it was clear that Walker was trying to appeal to his generation.

Why would people his age celebrate a car that was being phased out of the American marketplace when they were still in diapers? "Because our parents owned them," said Walker, who exhibited his '58 Euro ragtop and a '58 black convertible. His Vee Dub friend Mark added, "Because the cars represent youth. When I'm in one, I feel a youthful spirit."

"Not too long ago, five of us drove our Beetles down to Los Angeles," Walker said. "It felt like we were in a cult."

"Yeah, people were flashing us the peace sign and yelling for us to pull over," Mark said. "When I'm on the freeway and I see another Beetle, I drive right up alongside it."

"Young people are attracted to Volkswagen Beetles because they don't need a big wallet to restore one," said Walker.

As if on cue, Walker chimed in and reminded everyone that the meet was going to end soon so that he and his Bug buds could pack up and form a fleet of old-timers to cruise out to the beach for the rest of the afternoon.

The younger generation has always been fascinated with the Bug. In the sixties and seventies, lots of high school students mastered the twists and turns of their hometown backroads in Volkswagen Beetles. The car was cheap to buy, inexpensive to run (in those days gas was slightly more than a quarter a gallon) and hip to drive. At Nottingham High School in Syracuse, New York, a group of Bug pals decided to band together into an officially sanctioned school club. Their advisor was a cool social studies teacher who owned a Beetle. The club even made it into the 1971 yearbook. "All us kids who drove Bugs to school parked together," said Terri Gerber, club president known then as Rube to her Vee Dub cohorts. They went everywhere together, including drive-ins after jamming as many friends as would fit into their Bugs. "Our cars were pretty rickety, but we always managed to get around. If a Bug didn't start, we had our hair dryers ready to get the moisture out of the distributor."

In the yearbook photo, Gerber is in the foreground sitting in the sunroof of her '64 Bug. She and her club mates are making the VW sign with their hands: V with two fingers of the left hand and W with three fingers of the right hand. "We were a bunch of wanna-be hippies," Gerber said. "We were a bit too late, but our VWs definitely brought us together—a camaraderie that wouldn't have existed if it weren't for our Bugs."

●

*Vintage-Beetle drivers converged on a grassy knoll in California's Santa Clara Valley.*

In 1967,
the Beetle increased
from a weakling forty
horsepower to a
buff fifty-three, from a
six-volt battery to
twelve.

# *mechanical reasoning*
# Bug Fixation

**W**hen viewed through rose-colored glasses, the Volkswagen Beetle appears ultra-reliable, running for hundreds of thousands of miles without a hitch. Remove the glasses and you see reality. A Bug, like any other car, breaks down, often at the most inopportune times and in the most undesirable places. Most Vee Dub owners know this all too intimately. But that's one of the reasons why the Bug generated such a faithful following. Because it was relatively easy to fathom mechanically, even owners spooked by dealing with their car's hardware could grow to be on intimate terms with it. If you understood what made the Bug tick—and stop ticking—you could become seriously attached to it. A little mechanical know-how stretched a long way with the Beetle.

Of course, a Bug can also be a curse. A simple part like a distributor rotor breaks on a lonely stretch of country road, and you're forced to hitchhike to civilization. A throttle cable snaps in the thick of rush-hour traffic and not only is your life in peril, but the car itself becomes the commuter curse of the day until a tow truck arrives.

But like faithful pets, Bugs have also pulled off miracles, hanging on for dear life when by all reason they should have succumbed. How often have Beetles arrived at a destination on a wing and a prayer? The Bug putts its way over thousands of miles on a cross-country jaunt only to give up the ghost on its landing. The starter expires? A gentle push to pop the clutch and a quick trip to a local Bug doc gets you back on the road. Or the engine blows on a long, multi-lane bridge. Does the Bug let you down? No, it sputters on three cylinders, until it clears the span, then shutters and bites the dust in a safe breakdown lane. What to do? Call a tow truck and reward the car with a new motor.

Beetles undergo mechanical glitches—bugs, of sorts—that need attention from time to time. In its heyday, because it was the car best suited to drivers with empty wallets, towing its carcass to a garage often wasn't an option. Reluctantly, you

*Bugs awaken: Beetles were mass-produced on the Wolfsburg assembly line, circa 1960s.*

were forced to work on the Bug yourself. You didn't plan on being intimate with your Bug, exploring its inner workings and unlocking the deep mysteries of its personality. But if you had to get back on the road, you were forced to plumb those depths, even if you flunked mechanical reasoning aptitude tests in high school.

Out of necessity, hundreds of Bug owners (myself included) were transformed from absolute no-brains with wrenches to mechanically-enlightened dolts who could at least adjust valves and replace a fan belt thanks to the inspired guidance of John Muir. In 1969, the late Vee Dub mechanical guru authored the ever-popular repair book *How to Keep Your Volkswagen Alive—A Manual of Step-By-Step Procedures for the Compleat Idiot*. (John Muir Publications, Santa Fe, New Mexico) His philosophy? To truly become one with your car, you must get down and greasy. Your Buggy ain't running? Well, get into a Zen space of motoring maintenance and pull out the metric wrenches.

Muir succeeded in making thousands of Beetle owners mechanically literate and sufficiently adept to grab a tool and mix it up with the car's nuts and bolts. Bugs were the perfect testing ground for taking a dip into the esoteric world of mechanics because they were one of the easiest car models to work on. Sometimes all it took to get a disabled Beetle back on its feet was an afternoon's worth of noodling with loosened battery cables, fouled spark plugs or rusted screws before getting to the heart of the ailment. And Muir knew exactly how a lamebrain could botch a simple procedure like a tune-up, cautioning against doing something thick like mixing up the correct order of the spark plug wires. You've done the job, but instead of power you get copious backfiring? Seek Muir's wisdom for your answer and then let him hold your hand to undo your blunder.

Having the ability to work on your Beetle was worn as a badge of honor. Yet what about the real hard jobs? Don't waste your time. Call in the Vee Dub experts, like Berkeley

> Beetles had split rear windows until 1953, when the oval window made its debut. The oval gave way to the big rear window in 1958.

mechanic Ken Shapiro, owner of Precision Peoples Car Repair. He's got Bugs in his blood.

His story begins in 1969, at the height of the sexual revolution, when he was living in Boston. He was having a good time, driving around in a cool purple and green VW bus. "Everyone back then in my generation either had a van or a Beetle," he recalls. "We were either getting stoned or doing mushrooms in them and going to the anti-war rallies in Boston Commons."

Shapiro worked as an aircraft mechanic but was laid off in 1970. He used to frequent a VW dealership on Charles Street at the bottom of Beacon Hill for van parts. He noticed there was a bunch of counterculture types working there. When his money ran out and he needed a job, he inquired at the garage. At his old job, there was a dress code. At the VW shop, everyone was a hippie with long hair.

The freaky-looking Shapiro was hired and worked his first VW tour of duty. A couple of years later he and a friend from the shop decided to head for California where they figured they could open their own VW repair garage because the cars didn't rust there. They were tired of working on Bugs in Boston, where if the car was over two years old, you had to use a torch to pry things apart.

So the pair hit the road in Shapiro's '58 Bug, which was still in decent shape because it had been stored in a garage during the winter. They made it to California via Mexico City, putting ten thousand miles on the faithful Beetle. When they arrived in Berkeley they opened up a shop with a thousand-dollar loan and prepared for the Bugs to roll in. They didn't have to wait long.

"There were millions of Beetles in Berkeley," Shapiro recalls. "The cars were so ugly they enjoyed a cult status here." In other words, the nonconformist types that were attracted to the university town also loved the Bug.

In his shop, there's a black-and-white photo on the wall near the front counter of a long-haired Shapiro and his equally hippie-looking partner at their shop where they charged eight dollars an hour for labor, an incredibly bottom-basement price even in those years. "We had all the right attributes for VW mechanics in Berkeley. We were cheap, we had long hair and we smoked weed." However, six months later the partnership fizzled. Shapiro bought his friend out for five hundred dollars and has been personally responsible ever since for keeping thousands of Bugs alive and well in the San Francisco Bay Area.

While for years his shop dealt exclusively with Volkswagens, in the early eighties Shapiro had a change of heart.

Many of his old customers were selling their VWs and buying new Japanese cars, which had become popular in the late seventies. He got tired of hearing clients ask him if he could work on their new cars. He threw in the greasy towel. "We had already broken the ice of working on water-cooled cars when Volkswagen Rabbits came off the line in 1975," he recalls. "Well, by 1978, we were deep into Rabbit shit around here already, so I figured we could also take on Japanese cars."

If you detect a note of disgust in Shapiro's words when talking about post-Bug Volkswagen, it's because he's not partial to the new lines of VWs. He also complains that the auto maker put out inferior products for years before the

*Bug details: a kitty asleep at the wheel, left; the speedometers, above.*

Bug's official end. "Back in Boston we didn't see a lot of old cars," he says. "Most were two or three years old because Bugs didn't last longer than five or six years because they rusted out. When I moved out here it was common to see '56 and '57 Bugs. They were so simple to work on. I love the design of the original Beetle. There wasn't anything you couldn't fix in a couple hours. You could overhaul an engine or replace a transmission in a day. The newer models weren't as well made."

Shapiro is certainly no VW zealot. He still loves the old design and maintains that Porsche was a true genius for coming up with the prototype Bug. But it's

been a long time since he's owned a Bug of his own. In fact, in the mid nineties he sold an ancient '54 that had been sitting in his shop for years. The buyers were a couple of eager teenagers looking for a project. "They were like those guys in the film *Raiders of the Lost Ark* when they thought they found the ark," Shapiro says.

He figured the car was the three thousandth Bug sold in the U.S. It was a basket case, meaning that there were pieces of the car scattered around the shop in different baskets. But it was ninety percent complete. Shapiro had simply lost interest. So he placed an ad in the newspaper, got fifteen calls right away and sold it on the spot for fifteen hundred dollars. In the next week, he received fifty more calls and

*The distributor caps, left; even a Bug at rest, above.*

# John Muir's Beetle Wisdom

$\mathcal{N}$ uggets of car-talk wisdom John Muir matter-of-factly passed on in his book *How to Keep Your Volkswagen Alive—A Manual of Step-By-Step Procedures for the Compleat Idiot* (John Muir Publications, Santa Fe, New Mexico):

• "A quick way to ruin a VW is to put detergent oil in after non-detergent oil has been used for awhile."

• "The morning warm-up is the nicest thing you can possibly do for your engine."

• If your starter is not working, "...the starter gear may be hung up in the flywheel, which happens from time to time. Turn off the key, put the car into third gear and push it backwards to unlock the starter assembly from the flywheel gear."

• Don't use jumper cables from one battery to another for fear of ruining the fuel-injection system in later modeled Bugs. Muir warns, "Fuel injection car owners had better prepare to have a well-charged battery in their cars at all times."

• To prolong the life of the Bug, oil changes and valve adjustments should be done every three thousand miles or if freeway driving is involved every fifteen hundred miles.

• One of the more informative pieces of advice from past readers of his book: "Another reader was checking his fuel pump and his buddy turned the engine over causing a spark. [He] told us (precisely) how long it takes a Bug to burn (remarkably fast)," Muir adds. "So, please, *don't make sparks around gasoline*—right?"

*Previous spread: Ken Shapiro, left, Ron Blinn and his dog Bush took time out at their fix-it shop in Berkeley, California, in 1972.*

figures he could have sold the Bug for twice as much.

Why did Shapiro lose his passion for the Bug? Part of it has to do with his daily intimacy with the car. But he also says that the basic Beetle design became outdated. Shapiro, who cut his hair in 1980, expresses a sentiment similar to many former owners: "People grow up. It's hard to fit two growing kids in the back seat of a Bug. Plus, compare one with any new car. It wouldn't take you long to tell which is better to drive. Having driven Bugs on extended trips over thousands of miles and having driven them through the dead of winter, I can say that they're not very good cars as far as creature comforts go."

One of the keys to Volkswagen's success in setting up dealerships in North America in the fifties was to ensure that parts and service were components to each operation. It was a lesson learned from earlier efforts of foreign car companies who imported their vehicles into the U.S. but neglected to bring mechanics up to speed on how to repair them. And if parts weren't readily available, well, who would want to buy an import? Volkswagen prided itself in stocking parts and providing service, which became integral elements of its marketing strategy in the sixties.

Years later, with the demise of the original Bug, Beetle owners must resort to other methods of maintenance. Increasingly, those committed to keeping their cars in running order scoop up junkers to be scavenged for spare parts. Then there's the old-fashioned junkyard. It used to be that you could wander through one with your own tools and wrestle parts from totaled vehicles. Now everything's computerized, which means you don't have to roll up your sleeves with WD-40 in tow.

Salvage yards that deal only with Volkswagens are rare but they do exist. Case in point: Bud's Bugs in Concord, California. Since the eighties, Bud has been deluged with owners seeking Bug bits. In addition to later modeled VWs, the shop has mostly '68 to '76 models, although earlier Beetles do occasionally show up. Bud, who's been providing a final resting place for wrecked Bugs on a three-quarters of an acre lot since the early seventies, is not the sentimental type when it comes to Beetles. People call, he says, when a Bug dies along a roadway. Plus, he's got a reputation with tow truck drivers who know that his lot is the best place to drag dead Beetle bodies.

If a cat has nine lives, a Bug has more. An inspiring tale of breathing new life into a Beetle comes from Proctor Academy in Andover, New Hampshire. The previously mentioned Yunus Peer not only taught modern foreign policy, Middle East history and sociology at the prep school, but also played Bug doc one semester. During the term breaks, Proctor faculty members change the pedagogical pace from rigorous academic studies to hands-on extracurricular projects. Peer sponsored a week-long Beetle makeover course in 1998.

Peer tracked down a beat-up '68 Beetle which he bought for five hundred dollars. A Beetle lover who had revitalized a couple of his own Vee Dubs, Peer did the preliminary work to get the car in workable shape, taking it to a metal shop for basic structural repairs. When he opened the course for enrollment, fourteen students signed up. Peer accepted ten, including three girls.

On March 15, his class entered the school shop and found a Bug shell on wheels with all the parts stripped and laid out for assembly. Within five days, the enthusiastic students nursed the car back to health. One kid rewired the entire vehicle, then put in a CD player with speakers in the kick panels. Others reupholstered the back seat. One Bugphile worked on parts in the Proctor machine shop. Peer invited Bug experts in as guest speakers. One mechanic had three students eager to help him put the motor in. A body work expert taught the kids how to buff the car properly.

At the end of the course, Proctor students proudly

displayed their finished product in the school auditorium: a '65 tornado red Beetle. "It brought the house down," recalls Peer.

Of course, the project conjured up new Bug stories. "The parents of one of the students involved in reassembling the car went on their honeymoon in a Beetle," says Peer, who has since moved to Hawaii with his family and started his VW treasure hunts anew. "They blew the motor and spent part of their honeymoon repairing it."

●

*Left and above: Corpses in a Bug grave-yard, Ludlow, Massachusetts. Opposite: Offering a momentary resting place for miles of wires, a worn-out Bug gently weeps in a Des Moines, Iowa, junkyard.*

6

Beetle beauty
is in the eye
of the beholder.

# car as canvas
# BugArt

**A** Bug is a blank canvas. For the creatively inclined, it calls out to be transformed into a work of art. One of the Bug's most redeeming qualities is its tolerance for enduring the most outrageous paint jobs and outlandish body modifications—without severe damage to its ego. Few other, if any, car types could bear the abuse.

It's almost as if the Beetle were designed to be made fun of, which is what many people do. They take an already animated car and make it even more cartoonish. A yellow Beetle with eyelashes painted around the headlights gets graffitied with psychedelic multicolored circles and slashes. A faded blue Bug acquires a new face with an additional set of eyes, bloodshot, on the hood. Some Bugs are a comic patchwork of hues—different colored doors and panels salvaged from less fortunate cars. Others are made into moving shacks. And of course during the sixties, the Beetle was dressed in any number of different outfits, ranging from flower-power hippie garb to real grass that required a regular hosing.

Then there are the mutant Beetles, those that have been tucked and pinched and recreated in various ways. Maybe the wheel wells are a little bigger than standard, maybe there's a dorky-looking fin on the hind side. A high school friend once owned a Beetle transformed into a hulking but ultimately unappealing wide-body. Inside the monster Bug with mag wheels were plywood cabinets and plush, seventies-cool, floor-to-ceiling shag carpeting.

There's an entire school of Bug modification called the Cal Look, which features lowered frames (the low-rider look), the de-chroming of all exterior body parts and more often than not high-decibel stereo systems. By far the ugliest makeover is that wanna-be '40 Ford grille or, even worse, a Rolls-Royce front end. It's way too pretentious for such a humble little vehicle.

Sophisticated car artistry using a Bug as the foundation block is a whole different story. Perhaps the most famous car artist is Harrod Blank, son of esteemed filmmaker Les Blank and a successful cinematographer in his own right. The younger

Blank's multicolored '65 Bug is decorated with spinning flowers, a TV set, a globe, rubber chickens, fake money glued to the rear end, a planet earth mailbox painted red, dozens of found objects and lots of other oddities. Plus there's that array of loud screaming sounds that emanate from it.

Blank's car is the star and inspiration for his documentary film and companion book, *Wild Wheels*, which showcases coast-to-coast auto art by eccentric people who have created flamboyant vehicles of self-expression. In the back Blank spotlights forty-six artistically-transformed cars including Cadillacs, Chevy vans, a Ford station wagon, and a couple pick-up trucks. But the car model most frequently exhibited is the Bug.

What makes a Bug such a good art project? Blank attributes the Beetle's success to its "ridiculous" appearance. It's funny, strange and totally different from any other car on the road. He also notes that until recently the Bug was inexpensive to buy. So why not play around with it? You don't have much to lose—in contrast to experimenting with a sports car like a Ferrari, which has a high resale value.

Blank was seventeen when he bought his '65 Bug. It was his way of saying that he didn't fit in with the rest of the world. It was a white car, which he found boring. How to make it more appealing? How about painting a rooster on the door? He got such a positive public response that he was inspired to continue experimenting artistically with the car.

Blank named his idiosyncratic artwork *Oh My God!* (his vanity license plate reads OMYGAWD) because that's what people say when they first see it. In making modifications (it's a constantly evolving work-in-progress), Blank has adopted an aesthetic compatible with the Bug's reputation as the People's Car. He says, "The Volkswagen is definitely not elitist. It's a down-home, home-grown kind of car."

The canvas for Blank's latest creation is yet another Bug. In 1998, he made over a '63 Beetle as a rock 'n' roll mobile called *Pico de Gallo*. His concept was to make the car look like it drove through a rainstorm of music. Records,

*Seeing beyond the road. Above: Procreating Beetles in ice. Opposite: The Bug maestro prepares to conduct Symphony for Winter Volkswagen, in E Flat Tire.*

Since opening in April 1985, Stiftung AutoMuseum Volkswagen in Wolfsburg has been visited by thousands of VW enthusiasts. The museum exhibits a brief pictorial historical overview of the Volkswagen story, a couple of videos on history and advertising, and most importantly dozens of restored cars, most of which are Beetles. (There are also vans, a couple Karmann Ghias, military vehicles and older cars from Audi's early Auto Union days.) Below are my top five favorite Beetles in the museum.

### 5. Der Weltmeister—The Champion

A relatively nondescript Beetle, this 1972 metallic blue Volkswagen was crowned the Champion when it rolled off the assembly line of the Wolfsburg factory in 1972. It was Beetle number 15,007,034, making the Bug the most successful car ever built. Previous production champ: the Ford Model T.

### 4. 1968 Wedding Beetle

This 1968 automatic Volkswagen has a white wrought iron body instead of a regular shell. It was handcrafted in Mexico and used by a couple as its wedding vehicle. When the museum first displayed the car, a huge white veil was hung from the ceiling over it.

### 3. 1964 Messina Volkswagen

On June 16, 1964, two Italians set sail across the Strait of Messina in Italy with their propeller-driven Beetle. They made the trip from Ganzirri to Cannitello in thirty-eight minutes. In 1984, the duo repeated the feat.

### 2. Ferdinand Porsche's 1938 split-window

This beautifully restored black car was the first Volkswagen. It was the designer's private car. It's the centerpiece of the museum's collection.

### 1. Adolph Hitler's 1938 convertible

Handcrafted by Porsche, this spiffy looking black Beetle convertible was presented to Adolph Hitler in 1938 as an early fiftieth birthday gift. It is one of twelve cars produced that year. It has black hubcaps and rims, short six-inch windshield wipers, a simple rear bumper, tiny rear brake lights and a horn hooked on to the front bumper. The car was in Bavaria at the end of the war and given to a doctor by the U.S. occupation army. The doctor drove the car over three hundred thousand miles before selling it to a dealer/car collector in Munich in 1955. He wrote down the chassis number and requested information from the factory, which traced the car back to Hitler. Before coming to Stiftung AutoMuseum Volkswagen, it was exhibited in a Munich museum.

Honorable mention: the four-door Volkswagen taxi, one of only thirty built in 1952 by the Berlin coach company Rometsch.

*1969-style Peace and Love: The wrought-iron Bug took to southern California streets with a flourish.*

CDs and various instruments are strewn on the hood and sides of the car. There's a stage on top of the car where musicians can perform. Its nickname is Whoa, Mama!, which is the first reaction Blank heard when he drove it.

Eric Staller, another Bug artist, unveiled his variation-on-the-Beetle in Manhattan, an appropriate setting for a car covered with dozens of rows of flashing synchronized lights (a total of 1,659) which blink in twenty-three computer-generated patterns. Staller's '67 Bug, the *Lightmobile*, is one of many in-motion, lighted sculptures he has created. His other "urban UFOs" include the *Bubbleboat*, a light-strewn raft that takes on the appearance of a spaceship when fully lit. It's not clear why Staller chose a Bug to make *Lightmobile*, but a good guess may have something to do with the car's size. Try doing this with a Cadillac and you'd need three times as many bulbs.

As strange as it may seem, wrought iron is the most popular medium for car art after paint. In *Wild Wheels*, Har-rod Blank profiled San Antonio, Texas, resident Joe Gomez, who explained that his creation, the *Wrought Iron VW*, came to him in a dream. In lieu of a regular body shell, his Bug has a body made of wrought iron fashioned in an arabesque design. It's a see-through car that he built by hand in nine months. Another wrought iron Beetle was made in Santa Barbara, California, and yet another was built in Mexico and used as a wedding car. The latter is housed at Stiftung Auto-Museum Volkswagen in Wolfsburg as part of its permanent car collection.

It took Ron Dolce eighteen years to complete his car art masterpiece *Marble Madness*, a.k.a. *The Glass Quilt* (thus the vanity license plate GLASQLT). It's a '69 Bug bejeweled with thousands of marbles and hand-applied wedges of stained glass. Also featured in *Wild Wheels*, *Marble Madness* is frequently seen in the San Francisco Bay Area. Every weekend and occasionally on weekdays, Dolce parks his motorized artwork in neighborhoods where there's lots of foot traffic and sells postcards of *Marble Madness*. When Beetle 2.0 was just beginning to make its appearance in the summer of 1998, Dolce joked to passersby that his car was the new Beetle.

*Marble Madness* certainly attracts crowds. On a Saturday afternoon in front of a popular coffeehouse in the Piedmont district of Oakland not far from his home, Dolce parked the car in a yellow zone and like a carnival barker peddled his postcards. Two elementary school-aged African-American kids rushed up to *Marble Madness* and gushed, "Tight!" One asked, "You make this?" You bet, Dolce replied. He asked them if their parents

would let them glue marbles onto their car. They shook their heads. "No way, but this is so tight!"

They started asking more questions, but the feisty Dolce interrupted. "Buy the postcard," he said, then shoved one of the oversized cards toward the kids. "See, the back has answers to all your questions." Sure enough, there's a list of FAQs (Frequently Asked Questions), which explains that the project started after a fender bender ripped off his bumper. He replaced it with a handmade bamboo one, then encountered another bump, this time on the front hood. That's when the marble fix began. Using a tube of silicone adhesive, he designed what turned out to be the first brush strokes of his *objet d'art*.

*The marble mosaic of Ron Dolce's* Glass Quilt, *left; a (bizarre) faced Beetle, above.*

In a city where uniqueness is commonplace, Michael Patchen's satin black Bug makes for a slightly ominous sight on the streets of Berkeley, California. Most Beetle car art takes on a whimsical nature. Patchen's '69 Volkswagen is subtly scary. It's a vampire Bug with fangs on the bumper, spikes on the hood, rectangular headlights, enlarged fenders, snakeskin-fake velvet upholstery, a skull gear shift, eight-ball door locks and a license plate that reads NOS4AH2 (Nosferatu, which is what the villagers always whispered in Dracula films when the Count was making his bloodthirsty rounds).

Patchen, a Bay Area Rapid Transit

train driver, is a fan of horror films and vampire culture. "I suppose I could have painted flowers on my car, but since I'm into the dark elements, I opted to do something different," he says. "I liked the idea of creating a Bad Boy. It looks bad with the fangs, spikes and big tires. But a Beetle can never be real evil and spooky. No matter what you do, bottom line it's still cute."

Volkswagen Beetles have been transformed into all sorts of bizarre and at times even grotesque artwork. Most of these cars with their bright colors and hey-look-at-me exhibitionism go over the top. Give me the Bug *au natural*, in different states of damage and disrepair. They're blue-collar works of art—pock-

*Harrod Blank's* Oh My God! *Bug, left; Bug with blood-shot eyes, above.*

90

*Yes, it's going to be a birthday party. But whose? The Bug's or a fourteen-year old kid's? Or one in the same?*

marked here and dimpled there, crinkled on one side and crumpled on the other.

Here's what I see as I spin around town: Bugs with one eye missing; wrinkled and protruding bumpers; a crushed fender painted with daisies; hood bonnets freckled with paint and flecked with rust; rear bumpers tilted downward in a frown, tilted upwards in a smile; nicks and splotches on the doors, the hood and the bald dome; sagging running boards; broken pilot windows; dangling exhaust pipes; engine compartment doors resting on the rear bumper.

Beauty is in the eye of the beholder. One man's junk is another's Bug art.

On the other hand, there's plenty of Bug allure when the cars are renovated back to their original state. That too is a fine art. Many Beetle owners spend their leisure time on work-in-progress restorations. It's a Bug party: a bath of fresh paint, a valise full of new parts and a suit of new upholstery. When it's coming-out time, the Beetle, all shiny and groomed, wheels out of the garage and takes to the streets. At once exquisite and charming, the Bug on its own terms becomes a masterpiece of the automobile world.

●

*Glue and paint, make a Beetle what it ain't. Above: Eric Staller flips the switch on his '67 Bug, the Lightmobile. Opposite: The Turf Bug fed by its owner. This garden variety Bug requires a lawn mower (separate purchase necessary).*

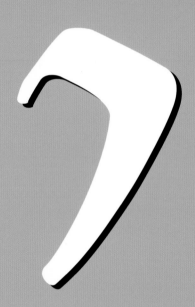

In the early
fifties, Volkswagen
gave gold watches to
owners of cars that
surpassed the
one-hundred-thousand
kilometer mark.

# keepsakes & trinkets
# BugToys

If you're a Bug fan, you no doubt have fond memories of the car even if you don't own one any longer. You may say that you're dying to someday buy one again—a second vehicle for getting around town, a backup for the starting car. Chances are you either won't find one or will be chased off by the exorbitant prices the precious little gems are commanding these days. That's a good thing because buying one can prove dangerous. Bugs like to breed. If Beetlemania does strike, you may be tempted to buy a mate or create an entire family of the cars. And if you're really bit by the Bug, well, that's when you build a barn or rent a large garage to house the stable.

But you can be an auto-less Bughead by collecting the plethora of Beetle memorabilia that comes in all sizes, shapes and colors. If you were in the market, you could pick up everything from wind-up toys and scale models (from Matchbox Bugs to cheap made-in-China Beetles) to toilet paper dispensers, lunch boxes, cookie jars, telephones, T-shirts and hats. In addition, while not as prosperous as the Mickey Mouse product line, lovable Herbie playthings continue to be strong sellers for Disney. The Franklin Mint offers scale model replicas of Beetles, including a classic sedan, a convertible and a peace-and-love Bug, with each car decorated in a unique flower-power design.

At the Volkswagen auto museum in Wolfsburg, Germany, you can buy dozens of postcards, Beetle-shaped erasers, platinum models, key chains, ties, umbrellas and bags of Bug-shaped black licorice. In the town that Bug built, you can find Beetle cake tins, gifts of chocolate decorated with tiny models and a cartoonish ladybug, as well as several books on the car in different languages.

In the first chapter of his novel *Still Life with Volkswagens* (The Overlook Press, 1995), Geoff Nicholson introduces the character Carlton Bax, who in addition to possessing a fleet of rare air-cooled Bugs, owns one of the world's foremost VW memorabilia collections.

Nicholson, who himself admits to dabbling in Bug stuff, sketches a comic setting where the Volkswagen is everywhere. Millionaire Bax wakes up, turns on his Beetle-shaped bedside lamp, looks at his Bug clock, takes a shower with soap molded to resemble the car, admires his huge collection of toys on display in his house and dresses in underwear with Bug motifs and a T-shirt with a cartoon Beetle dragster. In his billiards room he has rows of hubcaps and steering wheels displayed on the wall. His desk has Beetle stationary, ruler, tape dispenser, stapler, pencil sharpener and paperweight. At breakfast, he uses his Bug salt-and-pepper shakers, drinks coffee from Beetle mugs and flicks ashes from his cigarette, lit with a Beetle lighter, into a Beetle ashtray.

Bax plays so humorously because of his ad nauseam Beetle fanaticism. Nicholson delivers the ultimate punch line when he has Bax drive away, not in one of his many Volkswagens, but in a Range Rover. Why? Because, according to Bax, Volkswagens are cool to collect, but he doesn't relish driving one.

Real life Beetle hobbyists are plentiful. In Chicopee, Massachusetts, Arthur Needham has amassed hundreds of VW collectibles to complement his flock of real-deal cars. A self-professed "Bug freak," Needham got his first VW toy when he was seven years old and over the years fed his Beetle fever by going to flea markets and yard sales. Family members showered him with Bug gifts on his birthday and at Christmas, and even his boss at work was on the lookout for cool and unusual Beetle toys. Included in his collection are battery-operated Beetle playthings, a Bug bumper car

*Secret rendezvous: two toy bugs met on the railing of a deck that overlooks the City by the Bay.*

from a New York amusement park, a VW bumper-car game and a stuffed cat dressed in a T-shirt with a Bug motif.

In Phoenix, Arizona, Melissa and Jerry Jess have a mail-order business that deals in VW toys and collectibles. They offer plenty of toys (including rare Hong Kong-made plastic split-window vehicles from the fifties), *Herbie* View-master reels and movie posters, cookie jars, Hot Wheels Bugs, wood cutouts, stickers, magazines, books, video tapes, patches, a Frisbee-like Flying Disc with the VW logo and Volkswagen Christmas cards.

The Jesses fell into the VW collectibles business in 1979. "That's when I made the mistake of giving my husband a toy Beetle for Christmas," Melissa recalls. The Bugs proliferated as friends began giving Jerry other toys and items related to Volkswagen. Soon the pair started hunting for and buying vintage bug toys. In the early eighties there wasn't much memorabilia available, but they didn't give up the search. Instead, they were joined by friends, including

one couple that decided to move and sell their collection. Melissa and Jerry bought it before realizing they had purchased a lot of duplicates. That's when they started selling. Since then, the Jesses report, it's easier to be a collector because of an avalanche of new Beetle toys and objects.

In San Jose, Bug enthusiast Ray Schubert has amassed a two-thousand-piece collection of memorabilia. He regularly attends Volkswagen-related events where, at the very least, he buys a commemorative T-shirt. He owns hundreds of them. His toy collection is bursting at the seams with everything from a coin-operated Bug to tiny Bug trinkets barely visible to the naked eye. Even though he's inundated with Beetle stuff, he's constantly watching for new Bug knickknacks. Schubert, who (no surprise) owns the Volks Authority garage, admits that he feels like he's gone a little overboard. But, that's the price you pay, he says, adding, "VW culture really is like a religion to me."

8

The newby
shares only two
characteristics with the
old-timer: rear passenger
assist straps and the
arc-like curve of the
rear roof.

# *beetle redux*
# BugNewby

**T**he Germans have a saying: everything has an end—only the wurst has two. With the advent of Beetle 2.0, perhaps that proverb should be amended: only the wurst *and* the Bug.

It was the first day of spring 1998 when several Bay Area Volkswagen dealers assembled on Justin Herman Plaza at the Embarcadero in San Francisco to pick up their brand new models. A hundred yards away, near the bay-front Ferry Building, a car carrier with several factory-fresh autos was being unloaded. Excited passersby snapped photos while curious drivers craned their necks to catch a glimpse of the mysterious cargo. There, in newly minted condition, was Beetle 2.0, which already had garnered a reputation as a darling of the motoring press since its debut at the Detroit car show in January.

At the Plaza, Volkswagen of America showcased a fleet of the new Beetles, their doors and hatchbacks open for view. A group of elementary school kids on a field trip ogled the adorable new cars. It proved to be more fun for them than a jungle gym as they climbed behind the steering wheel and crawled into the back seat.

Not one old Bug was in sight, but it was foremost in the memories of those old enough to have been intimately involved with one. A swarm of tourists interrupted their sightseeing duties to behold, sniff and caress the new edition. The sight of this latest Bug triggered several recollections of Beetles past: embarking on impromptu cross-country trips, cruising around town for hours on an empty gas gauge, enduring frigid winters with no heat and resorting to improvisational engine repairs with baling wire to salvage a vacation.

On the brink of pulling up stakes in the American automobile market because of sluggish sales, Volkswagen of America bet its future on the nostalgia card, harking back to the good old days when the Beetle was King. Though some high-ranking company officials had vowed to never look back to the bygone era of the Bug (it was unceremoniously retired in the American marketplace in 1979), other Volkswagen execs pushed ahead, paving the way for the new Beetle. They believed that this new Bug—a modern offspring of the heralded old body type—would help to jump-start VW's comeback in the auto world.

At the luncheon following the Embarcadero exhibit, one Volkswagen executive noted that while the old Beetle appealed to the youth of late sixties-early seventies San Francisco, the upscale, late nineties model was being shopped to a new market: the nouveau rich of Silicon Valley. That's where many ex-hippies traded in their bell bottoms and ratty Bugs for fashion jeans and sturdy BMWs—transforming themselves into silicon-chip entrepreneurs, founding computer and multimedia companies, combining progressive political ideals with business savvy and, ultimately, cashing in on the high-tech new economy.

Also attending the luncheon were reps from Arnold Communications, the Boston-based advertising agency that launched the witty "hug-it-drive-it?" ad campaign for the new Beetle with such clever epigrammatic sayings as "If you were really good in a past life, you come back as something better" and "If you sold your soul in the eighties, here's your chance to buy it back." Posterboard placards with examples of the print ad and billboard campaign were propped up around the room. A video with Bug footage from the psychedelic sixties and glimpses of the new Beetle TV ads (that debuted two days later on television's *The X-Files*) drove home the point that the old entomological specimen had indeed metamorphosed into a newfangled beauty.

Much like the original, the new car sports a whimsical, arch-like geometric design (position an elderly Bug alongside a newby and you see the profile of the rear curvature is identical) and a 'toon-like appearance that possesses an uncanny ability to make onlookers smile. But upon driving a new Beetle, the comparisons between it and its predecessor skid to a halt.

Comedian Jerry Seinfeld appeared with the prototype of the newby on the cover of *Automobile* in May 1994.

In showroom parlance, the new Beetle has sports-car punch from a two-liter, four-cylinder engine with one hundred and fifteen horsepower giddyup under the front hood and a tachometer on the interior instrument panel. The speedometer maxes out at one hundred forty (compared to my first car, a '61 Beetle, which topped out at ninety). The born-again Bug has a dual-toned horn instead of a beep, two-speed windshield wipers that do the job, brakes that work without pumping, instant toasty heat, driver and passenger air bags and the roomy, classy interior of a late-modeled auto (including a deep-welled dash that stretches from the steering wheel to the aerodynamic windshield, heatable front seats and two power outlets). Plus, the warranty includes a twelve-year corrosion protection deal (no more rusted-out wheel wells). Gone are that distinctive burnt oil smell in the tin-can cab and the rat-a-tat engine sound. But look closely and one finds a few interior traces of the old Bug, particularly the rear passenger assist straps.

Like any newly arrived immigrant, Beetle 2.0 wasn't content to sit on the docks all day. Following lunch, dealers went for a spin in their brash young charges, led by a motorcycle police escort. Once in Union Square, the heart of downtown San Francisco, with sirens blaring, the police cleared the way for a horn-honking parade. The new Bug had arrived.

A couple of weeks later, when new Beetle sightings were still rare, I parked my faded clementine orange '74 Bug on the street and made room in the garage for a spanking new bright yellow Beetle, on loan for a week from Volkswagen of America's press fleet.

With nothing else on the road remotely similar, the cheery Beetle 2.0 was an instant luminary. Throughout the week, people reacted with smiles, laughs, thrown kisses, waves, and double takes. Driving one is like walking a big puppy, an acquaintance said. It's like driving in a toy, a friend

*The newby was named 1998 Car of the Year by* Motor Trend *magazine and 1999 North American Car of the Year by a panel of journalists at the North American International Auto Show. Its advertising campaign promoted the car with witty one-liners reminiscent of, but decidedly different from, earlier ads.*

The engine's in the front,
but its heart's in the same place.

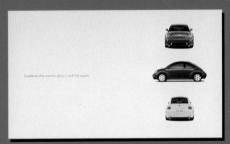

Suddenly the world's glass is half full again.

The new Beetle comes with a flower-power touch: a three-inch vase affixed to the dash.

remarked. It's the car of the future, my mechanic proclaimed.

On my first freeway jaunt, a Porsche zoomed up and the sporty driver of the Beetle's distant cousin flashed a big smile and gave the thumbs up sign before speeding off. Heading cross-town in Berkeley near the Ashby BART station, a droopy-pants high school kid pumped his fist into the air and yelled, "My first one!" Underneath the freeway in Albany where a construction crew was working, the hard hats didn't whistle but the yellow Beetle turned their heads.

At a red light on Bryant Street near the San Francisco police station, a hulking four-by-four utility vehicle with huge oversized wheels pulled up alongside. The twentysomething driver with a nose ring looked down, grinned and said he'd be game for a swap.

The new Beetle was a high-stakes gamble for Volkswagen. But because of dismal U.S. sales (in 1993 the automaker sold only forty-nine thousand cars, an anemic percentage of the import car market), a radical act was required. Otherwise it was *auf Wiedersehen* America. A year earlier, car designers at Audi, Volkswagen's corporate sister, began to discuss the possibility of reviving the Beetle and pumping new millennial life into the car that put Volkswagen on the map.

In Simi Valley, at Audi's California design headquarters shared with Volkswagen, Jay Mays, Audi's chief designer there at the time, got the wheels turning by selecting a group of designers from his team—including Freeman Thomas and Peter Schreyer—to secretively work on sketches and drawings of a new Beetle. Hartmut Warkuss, Audi's design chief in Germany, budgeted three hundred thousand dollars for further designs and scale models—a project that involved the entire Simi Valley Audi staff.

Audi designers were careful to leak no word to the design team working for Volkswagen, which, as a corporate entity, was firm in its mandate that the Beetle was best left dead. Resuscitating the Bug was equated with raising a

*Previous spread: The new Beetle made its San Francisco debut in a horn-honking parade to Union Square.*

# Beetles of Many Hues

The Nazi regime's KdF-wagen was billed as the People's Car. According to the contract people received when they began their layaway plan to purchase one of the factory fresh autos, the car would only be available in one color: a uniform-like deep blue-gray.

A sampling of Bug colors in the sixties: Panama Beige, Java Green (dark green), Bahama Blue (light blue), Sea Blue, Black, Pearl White, Anthracite Gray, Ruby Red.

In the eighties, Beetles came from the factory in Mexico in a variety of splashy colors, including Silver Metallic, Lime Green, Clementine, Topaz Metallic, Mars Red, Alpine White, Diamond Silver, Lemon Yellow, Chrome Yellow, Florida Blue, Barrier Blue, River Blue, Bahama Blue Metallic and a rare special edition Triple Black.

The new Beetle made its debut in four non-metallic colors (white, red, black and yellow) and four luminous metallic options (silver, bright blue, green and dark blue). In the car's first year of production, Volkswagen vastly underestimated how popular silver (a time-consuming color to paint) and yellow (a rare car color in North America) Beetles would be. Production did not meet demand which resulted in shortages and customer waitlists. In a September 11, 1998, *New York Times* article on the color scarcity, one new Beetle customer noted that while most of the colors made the car resemble a toy, the new silver Beetle looked both retro Art Deco and Jetson-like futuristic.

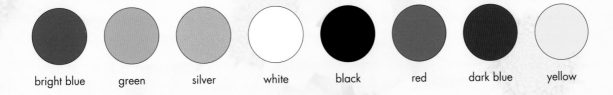

bright blue    green    silver    white    black    red    dark blue    yellow

white flag. Even though VW designers were often intrigued by the new Audi project, they had no clue that a new Beetle was being born right under their noses. The creation of Concept 1, as it was called by the Audi team, was based on three key characteristics of past Bug life—simplicity, reliability and honesty. The designers added a fourth quality, originality, which was crucial to insuring that the new car not be a rehash of the old.

On January 1, 1993, Audi chief executive Ferdinand Piech, grandson of Ferdinand Porsche, the original Beetle designer, assumed control of Volkswagen/Audi worldwide operations. Several months later Warkuss, who had surreptitiously funded the Concept 1 project and later gave the enthusiastic go-ahead for a full-scale model of the car, was promoted to design chief of Volkswagen/Audi. His new power base gave him the clout necessary to pull off the impossible and take Beetle 2.0, no longer a top-secret project, one step closer to production. Piech gave his approval to have Concept 1 unveiled at the 1994 Detroit auto show to get a barometer on public opinion.

The yellow prototype show car, jointly developed by both the Audi and VW design teams in Simi Valley, was an unqualified hit. Even so, it took several months before the project was given an official green light to proceed. Engineers decided to use the VW Golf chassis as the Beetle's guts, which required the car to be slightly longer than the prototype. Once the car's whimsical body was tweaked to fit the Golf platform, production was set into motion at Volkswagen's Puebla, Mexico, plant.

The hype surrounding Concept 1 combined with a revitalized marketing strategy and dealer discounts helped Volkswagen recover from its American sales slump. In 1997, the car maker sold one hundred and thirty-eight thousand cars, nearly tripling its sales from four years earlier. In the first eight months of 1998, Volkswagen sold one hundred fifty-two thousand cars, thanks in large part to the immense success of the new Beetle, which generated waiting lists across the U.S.

*Unsure of the newby's reception, Volkswagen set a modest first-year production run of 50,000.*

Shortly after Beetle 2.0 hit the street, the car garnered great press, especially for its safety features—not exactly the strong suit of the old Bug. In reporting on the new Beetle's top grade in slow-speed crash tests, the Associated Press wrote, "The Bug isn't only cute, it's tough." Among other small car competitors, the new Beetle sustained the least amount of front and rear bumper damage. A month later, the car was rated the safest car in the small-car class in high-speed crash tests administered by the Insurance Institute for Highway Safety in Virginia. In two forty-mile-per-hour crashes, the Bug scored higher than all other cars, including the Honda Civic, Toyota Corolla and Ford Escort.

Even a minor glitch like a recall to correct a wiring problem that could lead to stalling or engine compartment fires didn't sour the public's enthusiasm for the new Volkswagen.

While the old Bug was priced for the low-income crowd, the first crop of new Beetles was not cheap. Rock-bottom sticker price for a bare-bones Beetle was fifteen thousand two hundred dollars while full-option models were hiked up into the low and mid twenty thousand dollar range. (In contrast, thirty years earlier a new Bug sold for less than two thousand dollars, roughly the equivalent of ten thousand 1998 dollars when adjusted for inflation.)

Since production for year one was modest (only fifty thousand cars) and because they proved to be a big consumer hit, in many areas prices were inflated. Scalpers even circled like buzzards as people wait-listed were willing to bid extra in their attempt to purchase coolness.

The new yellow Beetle I had on loan proved to be a winner with my mechanic Ken Shapiro, who had personally sworn off Beetles several years earlier. He immediately branded it Year 2000 Car, then a moment later did what all good mechanics do when they meet any four-wheeler for the first time: he popped open the hood and checked out the new Bug's guts. Great engine, Ken said. Next he scoped out the back seat, remembering the old days when he just about lived in them. Lots of room, he noted, but could see that a big bump would probably result in passengers banging their heads on the ceiling.

Out on the highway, Ken gave the car thumbs-up on how it handled, especially the oomph in third gear. "Overall, I love this car," he said when we returned to his shop. "It's peppy, got great throttle response and it feels tight. It's definitely not an old car from the seventies. It's a nineties car."

While some Bugheads praised the new Beetle, just as many others condemned it as a yuppie impostor. While the old version was the People's Car, an inexpensive and reliable auto the blue-collar community could relate to, Beetle 2.0 was born an instant celebrity. It's an adorable car, but humility isn't one of its traits. It loves to be in the spotlight.

Owners of old Bugs drove them proudly, enduring the unpleasantries of foul weather and cold feet. Quite the opposite is true for the newby. Many new Beetle owners see their buggies as a status symbol. Along with the little extras like alloy wheels comes social prestige.

Word from Massachusetts, where Bugs were laid to rest long ago, is that the reborn Beetle became an upscale superstar. Not all reviews were sweet talk though. A family with a big garage took to parking the new Beetle in the driveway. The cute car, too obviously on display, incited neighbors to brand the owners show-offs.

However, Bug diehards need not fret. No matter how successful the new Beetle becomes, it will never replace the old. Even though one of the new ads for the newby stated, "A car like this only comes around twice in a lifetime," it won't resonate with its owners in the same way its elder did. It may have an idiosyncratic, Beetle-esque appearance and it may garner a cult following, but it won't become as omnipresent on the highway as the old-timer was in its prime. Times have changed.

The Volkswagen logo was designed circa 1937 by Francis Xavier Reimspiess, an engine designer working for Porsche.

## creating an icon
# BugPlugs

In the late forties when Volkswagen first contemplated exporting the Beetle to the United States, it was faced with a formidable task: how to foist a German-made car on an American public still reeling from horrific memories of World War II? Selling the Beetle was a marketing nightmare. Not only was it an automobile built by a recently vanquished foe, but the Beetle was the noxious Führer's own beloved babe. Can one imagine companies trying to hawk a Saddam Hussein all-terrain, luxury-sport utility vehicle, hustle a line of Charles Manson dune buggies or peddle a Theodore Kaczynski Unabomber brand manual typewriter?

Yet, only a few years after the demise of Hitler, his offspring came to America dressed in a little Bug's clothing. Volkswagen was here, but could it last? The goal was to spark a romance between two former enemies.

In 1948, Heinz Nordhoff, newly appointed industrial manager of the Volkswagen factory in Wolfsburg, cast his eyes on the United States as a potential market. His aim was practical: he needed U.S. dollars to secure American-made machinery for the factory. At the time, only a few stray Beetles had made their way into the States after vets in the post-war occupation army returned home toting their four-wheeled souvenir trophies.

To win over Americans, Nordhoff enlisted Ben Pon, a Dutchman who had overcome the odds and sold Beetles in Holland—no mean feat given that country's suffering under Nazi occupation. Pon arrived in New York on January 17, 1949, with a showroom model of the VW sedan in the hold of the Holland-America Line's M/S *Westerdam*. The American media immediately damned it as Hitler's car.

After meeting with similar responses from dealerships he was trying to woo, Pon raised the white flag, sold the car to cover his expenses and returned to Nordhoff with the bad news. Not to be dissuaded, Nordhoff himself came to the United

States later that year, carrying with him a batch of photographs instead of the real thing. However, he too was met with negative press and derision by potential importers.

In 1950, Max Hoffman, a New York foreign car dealer, was granted exclusive rights to import Beetles into the eastern United States. While his primary interest was in selling expensive autos like Porsches and Jaguars to dealers, Hoffman also agreed to sell Beetles, often offering them as bonus cars in package deals involving the fancier models. In fact, dealers found they could procure the sports cars easier if they also accepted the less desirable Beetles.

"Charles!"

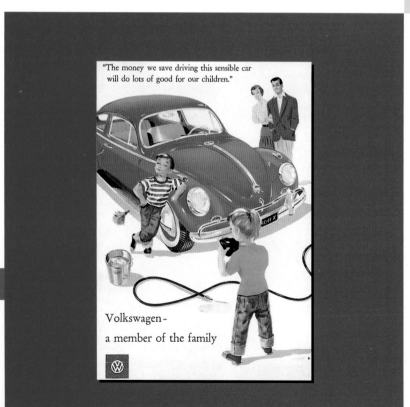

"The money we save driving this sensible car will do lots of good for our children."

Volkswagen – a member of the family

In 1950, the first year of official United States sales, three hundred thirty Beetles were sold, a minuscule share of the booming auto market of six hundred sixty million new car sales. At first an oddity on the highway, the peculiar-looking pipsqueak slowly gained popularity. Dealers began to specifically request Beetles primarily because customers were attracted to their relative low cost. By 1953, sales increased to fourteen hundred cars, still a dismal volume but encouraging enough for Volkswagen to establish headquarters in both San Francisco and New York with factory reps at the helm.

A pivotal year proved to be 1954. A former fighter pilot in the German Luftwaffe, Will van de Camp was charged by

*Early ads accentuated the car's economy for the all-American family, left.*

Volkswagen to take sales to the next level. He was the right man for the job as Walter Henry Nelson in his book *Small Wonder* explains: "Will van de Camp was an evangelist, possessed of a near-fanatic missionary zeal. He believed passionately in the Volkswagen and in the truth, beauty, and justice of his company's policies; he never doubted for a second that Volkswagen would become a tremendous success in the United States; he regarded it as heresy for a dealer to believe in (much less sell) any other car but the VW; and he considered it his personal mission in life to infect others with his faith."

Van de Camp was responsible for

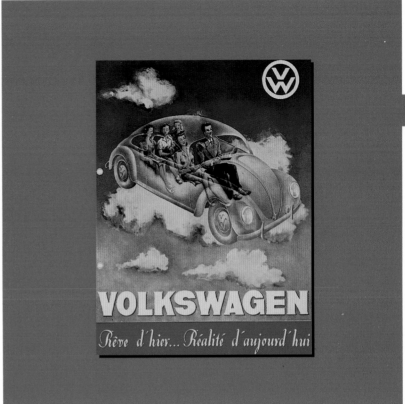

"They certainly make those Volks' airtight."

transforming Volkswagen in the United States from a hodgepodge distribution operation to an organized national system of dealer franchises. In 1955, over thirty thousand Beetles were sold. Forging a customer-friendly organization that emphasized a combination sales-with-service approach (making parts readily available and training repairmen in VW mechanical know-how), van de Camp laid the groundwork for what would eventually become Volkswagen of America, the biggest and most powerful foreign auto company to do business in the United States. By the time van de Camp's tenure ended in 1958, Beetle annual sales had mushroomed to one hundred thousand.

Under van de Camp's leadership,

*A French ad espoused a promise: "Yesterday's dream…today's reality," above.*

**Think small.**

**Will we ever kill the bug?**

advertising was a low priority. When Carl Hahn took over in 1959, marketing the quirky car via ads became an imperative despite the fact that the German factory could not keep up with existing orders. Even though in the late fifties there was an increased demand for foreign-made cars and low-cost compacts, the American buying public in general did not hold the Beetle in high esteem. In fact, some auto pundits deemed the car a passing fad. Plus, in some areas of the United States, the Beetle's reputation as the Hitlermobile was still alive and well.

Nevertheless, one hundred twenty thousand sedans were sold in 1959, making it the most popular foreign car on the American market. Part of that mass market success can be attributed to the car's quality and affordability. But the Madison Avenue ad agency of Doyle Dane Bernbach (known later as DDB Needham) deserves major credit. Hired in 1959 to institute the ad campaign for the Beetle, DDB with its humorously "honest" advertisements not only charmed the American public, but it also broke ground for a new era of creative marketing in the advertising world.

Instead of masking the car's shortcomings, DDB capitalized on its foibles with such frank, self-deprecating and amusing sayings as "Ugly is only skin deep" (implying that there's more car under the homely shell than meets the eye) and "Think small" (i.e., size doesn't matter when it comes to performance). Instead of the same glitzy images and cartalk prattle that characterized the auto advertising of the day, DDB's witty ads had simple layouts: a catchy, sometimes even arresting saying, an unglamorous photo of the car (and in the case of one of DDB's most famous ads on the immutability of the model from one year to the next, no photo at all) and a few paragraphs of cleverly written copy espousing the car's humble assets.

In one classic ad geared for hip audiences, the Beetle is identified as "Lemon." A close read of the small print reveals that the pictured car flunked its factory inspection because of a blemished chrome strip on the glove compartment. The ad plays on the car-lemon association, peeling the rind inside out to bolster the car's image. In essence, the ad guaranteed that because of Volkswagen's quality control its factory flukes never made it to the showroom. The punch line comes at the end: "Volkswagen plucks the lemons; you get the plums."

One marketing approach explored the unique outlook Beetles buyers were willing to adopt, as in an ad that shows a tiny Beetle with the caption "It makes your house look bigger." The ad goes on to explain that being a compact may have its disadvantages, but small is beautiful when it comes to finding a place to park, driving down narrow roads and returning from the gas pump with extra dollars in your pocket. In an amusing way, the reader is offered a nugget of advice: "Cars are getting to be bigger, so houses are going to look smaller. But one little Volkswagen can put everything back in its proper perspective."

A common theme in DDB's ads focused on the Volkswagen Beetle's outward appearance remaining virtually unchanged over the years (excluding, of course, the evolution of the rear window from split to oval to full in the fifties and the conversion from bumpers with overriders to one-piece bumpers in 1968). A mid sixties ad features a Beetle getting a paint job with the caption "How to make a '54 look like a '64." The answer: paint. The sell: Volkswagen makes changes to help the car run better, not to enhance its image. The wisdom: "So, if you like, you can keep your Volkswagen running forever. Just spray it every few years. Old paint rides again."

The less-is-more philosophy was offered in one ad that presented only a horizontal line with a distinctively Beetlesque curve. The pun-ish question: "How much longer can we hand you this line?" The modest answer: "Forever, we hope." The koan-like lesson: "Some cars keep changing and stay the same. Volkswagens stay the same and keep changing."

The clever advertising campaign effectively completed

*The early German ad campaign, left, contrasted with the now-classic Doyle Dane Bernbach ads in America, which represented the turning point of a new era of creative marketing.*

*Spanking new Beetles await buyers at a VW dealer lot, circa 1960s.*

the makeover of the Bug's image. Combining the car's increased popularity, in part due to its reliability, with America's penchant for long-term memory loss, Hitler's association with the car dissolved during the early sixties. Coinciding with the invasion from England of the rock 'n' rolling Beatles, the unassuming Beetle began to make a mark of its own as an American icon, a diminutive symbol of nonconformity, modesty and peace.

Doyle Dane Bernbach continued to represent Volkswagen until spring 1995 when Boston-based Arnold Communications beat heavy competition from several other ad agencies to score the Volkswagen of America account. While there was no Hitler figure to haunt the sales of the car, Arnold had its work cut out for it on another front: the company itself was rumored to be ready to pull up stakes in the North American marketplace because of sagging sales.

### The Bug Returns

Francis J. Kelly III, managing partner and chief marketing officer of Arnold Communications, remembers well the discussions within his agency when it was invited to compete for Volkswagen of America's advertising business in December 1994. After hashing through the pros and cons, Arnold decided to deliberately distance itself from VW's glory days, including the Bug. That was the secret to its success.

After an initial round of sixteen agencies presenting written proposals, Volkswagen officials paid a visit to the top eight contenders. Several ad companies put old Beetles in their lobbies or plastered the walls of their offices with Bug photographs as decorations to welcome the visitors. Kelly admits that some people at Arnold also considered that approach. But others countered that Volkswagen needed a new image—one that built on the past, but had a fresh delivery appropriate to the new cars. "So we didn't have a Beetle in sight," Kelly says.

Arnold won the account in April 1995 and in July

launched the Drivers Wanted campaign, with its catchy tag line, which helped to jumpstart Volkswagen of America's attempt to rebuild its business in North America. Even though Arnold's winning campaign focused on the cars Volkswagen was presently marketing (such as Golfs and Jettas), the firm also strategized how to launch the new Beetle, which at that time was still only in the Concept 1 prototype stage.

Detractors within Volkswagen feared that reviving the Beetle would take the brand backward, that the auto maker would once again be known only as the Beetle company. However, a combination of events gave the company the confidence to forge ahead. A key factor was that sales had begun to perk up in the United States. Then there was the car itself. It had the magic of the old Bug, but it was a modern, substantial automobile that met Volkswagen's standards.

Arnold went full throttle into developing its advertising campaign in spring 1997 when it became clear the new Beetle would make its debut at the Detroit Auto Show in January 1998. Led by managing partner and chief creative officer Ron Lawner, Arnold shifted into high gear and worked for ten weeks experimenting with different ideas. They presented the soon-to-be new Beetle to current Volkswagen owners and prospective buyers to get their responses. "The first reaction everyone had was to smile," says Kelly. "People approached the car slowly almost as if they were looking at a piece of art. It put a smile on their faces and joy in their hearts."

Arnold decided to reflect the new nature of the auto while genuflecting ever so slightly to its ancestor. "The new Beetle has the shape and the magic of the old car, but delivers it in a thoroughly modern automobile," says Kelly, who although he never owned a Bug had plenty of good memories in them, including his first underage behind-the-wheel experience. "Because the old Beetle was quirky, cheap and different, the people who liked it best were most often quirky and different. The new Beetle is unique, spir-

ited, fun. It's more for up-and-coming people who are in the middle of the action, not for a guy who wants to be different and stay on the outside. In order for Volkswagen to grow in North America, it can't be seen as a fringe brand. A lot of new Beetle buyers could purchase a BMW or a Mercedes, but they want to stay down to earth. They're successful, but don't want to be viewed as too serious or stuffy."

Arnold explored many options for packaging the Beetle for market. It finally settled on introducing the car by presenting a clean, unadorned image of it on a white page. The creative team found that the smaller the car appeared on the page the more its jewel-like shape could be appreciated. Then the ad writers developed punch lines about how it could be plugged into contemporary life. They also tapped into the emotional appeal of the past. Thus the headline: "The engine's in front, but the heart is in the same place."

Lawner and his crew developed several more one-liners and Arnold was in the driver's seat. The agency unveiled the campaign to Volkswagen of America management in Auburn Hills, Michigan, then reps hopped a plane to Germany and presented it to Volkswagen brass in Wolfsburg. It was met with enthusiastic approval. Originally, Arnold planned to launch the new Beetle with four or five ads, but the creative team came up with so many good one-liners, several ads with headlines targeting specific audiences were used. Some were what Arnold calls "core-brand messages" and included the classic headline, "If you sold your soul in the eighties, here's your chance to buy it back again."

Others were "buzzmakers," such as "Reverse engineered from UFOs." What in the world does that mean? "We believe if you do ten ads," Kelly replies, "you should include one or two that are edgy and fun enough that people will want to talk about them even if they don't completely understand the headline. The UFO one has a young attitude. We've found that a lot of Volkswagen loyalists love *The X-Files* and sci-fi books."

Arnold also made custon-fit ads. In *Boston* Magazine,

*In an image from an early sales brochure, note the elongated rendering of the compact car and the use of the word "limousine."*
*In contrast, Doyle Dane Bernbach's ads focused on honesty: you saw exactly what you got.*

DIE *Sonnendach* LIMOUSINE

# El Vochito on the Mexican Tube

at the Stiftung AutoMuseum Vokswagen in Wolfsburg, visitors can take a break from viewing the cars, sit down and tune in to a video of Bug TV commercials which were just as witty and entertaining as sprint ads. In addition to numerous commercials broadcast in the U.S., the video features television ads for Mexican audiences.

- A Clint Eastwood-type cowboy roams the range with his trusty horse. Together they ride over steep hills and ford deep streams. The grizzled cowboy then trades his companion in for a spanking new orange Beetle, which traverses through the same formidable terrain with ease.

- At a gala political event at the presidential palace, several diplomats arrive in expensive limousines to the cheers of the crowd. Then there's a beep-beep and a Volkswagen Beetle arrives. The police guard waves the car off. You're lost, he says. But El Presidente himself steps out from behind the wheel of the car and walks into the meeting.

- With the theme music from *Goldfinger* in the background, a James Bond lookalike gets into his high-tech car but is unable to get it started. The propellers for a water getaway turn on, the periscope pops up and the smoke screen machine fills the cab with fumes. Frustrated, Bond gets out of the car and presses a button on his high-tech wristwatch. Like a pet, a faithful Beetle arrives with a beep-beep and Bond drives off slowly.

- In a cartoon commercial, the Coyote takes on a Beetle instead of his archenemy the Road Runner. Of course, while trying to destroy the Volkswagen, the Coyote meets with similar calamities. After a few disastrous attempts, the crumpled Coyote gives up and the Beetle rides off nonchalantly issuing its Road Runner-like beep-beep.

the headline read: "Just what Boston needs, a car that stops traffic." In New York, underneath a picture of a yellow Beetle was the one-liner: "Cabbies will smile before they cut you off." In Hollywood, where cosmetic surgery is a lucrative business, the new Beetle ad read: "You can't even see the scars." One planned for Washington, D.C. featured a billboard with nothing on it except the headline "Stealth Beetle."

The simple image of the car with clever ad copy is reminiscent of the Doyle Dane Bernbach ad campaign in the sixties. Everyone at Arnold is well aware of those ads and considers them classics. "Doyle Dane Bernbach put together one of the greatest, if not *the* greatest, campaigns ever done," says Kelly. "It's what great creative is all about. The work is completely different; it's gutsy, smart, entertaining and highly effective. It not only helped to grow sales, but it made Volkswagen one of the most important and talked about brands in the nation. It made Volkswagen more than just a successful product; it became a part of American culture and an icon brand like Coke. But the new Beetle is no longer a weird, cheap and super-economical car. It's distinctive, substantial, driveable, fun, so we needed a modern marketing campaign that could be an equal of the brand's creative advertising heritage."

Arnold's strategy was to accentuate the elite appeal of the new Beetle, sold to a "mindset, not a demographic," as Kelly puts it in explaining why no people were featured in the first round of ads. "Age or class doesn't matter. We did not want to presuppose that you had to be a thirtysomething or wear hip shades to drive a Beetle. It's no longer the People's Car. It's a personal car. You can pick your color and fill it with your lifestyle."

*Ads for the newby are short on words, big on space.*

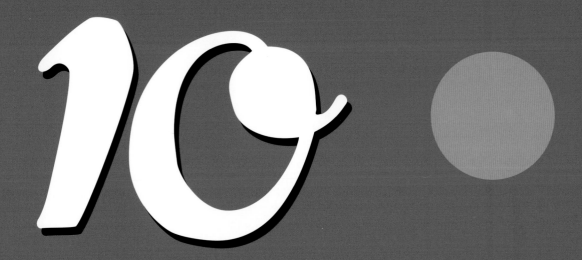

**10**

The Beetle
was built in Germany,
South Africa, Nigeria,
Australia, Brazil, Mexico,
but never in the
United States.

# *fans & pundits*
# BugCulture

In the sixties and seventies, the cult of the Volkswagen Beetle cut across a wide swath of society. The car endeared itself to young and old alike. Those who saw the glowing light of the radiant Bug and smelled its essence of burnt oil came from diverse backgrounds and experienced the auto in a variety of ways. Some Beetle fans moved on and bought new cars; many younger Bug lovers wish their parents never had gotten rid of theirs. While some ex-Beetlemaniacs still wax nostalgic about their old buggies, other drivers chalk up their Bug-transport days as a bygone era.

Then there's the GenXers, hip to all things retro. The powerful purchasing group has developed a whole new Bug fascination as they gravitate to the Summer of Love car.

In the sixties when protest was in the air and hippie-styled peace and love in vogue, Bugs were everywhere, especially at ground zero of the Free Speech Movement. David Lance Goines, a writer, artist and printer who runs St. Hieronymous Press in Berkeley, was a Free Speech activist at the University of California at Berkeley when he was expelled from the school for participating in demonstrations. He remembers the Bug days well. Back in the sixties, he drove a '62 black Beetle and reports that while it was difficult performing sexual acts in one, it wasn't impossible. "A lot happened in Volkswagens," he says. "Believe me, I know."

But Goines adds that making out in the back seat of a Bug wasn't that prevalent because the liberal sexual climate of the time didn't necessitate resorting to the use of a "mobile bedroom." Besides, the car just wasn't considered sexy. "In addition to having one for cheap transportation, the Beetle proved its best worth in providing shelter from inclement weather," says Goines.

He recalls that there were so many Bugs in Berkeley in the sixties that it wasn't uncommon to find oneself sitting in the wrong car. When he went to renew his car registration at the Department of Motor Vehicles, the woman who waited on him said that the city of Berkeley should be renamed Volkswagen because so many people there either owned Beetles or VW vans.

Goines says that the Beetle found favor with countercultural types because it was the essence of non-conformity, the Zeitgeist of the era. It also bucked the auto trends of the time; the other cars on the market were enormous dinosaurs that extolled power yet quickly became extinct when small cars took over. In stark contrast, the Bug kept the same outward appearance year in and year out. "There was an anti-status quality about the Beetle," says Goines, who owned one for twenty-five years before getting rid of his "death trap" in favor of a Volvo. "The Bug was definitely the auto of the times. It went against the demands of consumerism. It never went out of fashion. You couldn't say that about a '57 Dodge that looked absolutely silly in 1965. You assumed that if someone was driving a Volkswagen, he or she possessed the same temperament and anti-establishment sentiments as you."

Many Bugheads, unable to give up their allegiance to the car, have turned their thoughts to restoration. Once hailed for its cheap ride, the Beetle is deemed a class act that makes a strong showing in auto shows. It's come a long way from its Flower-Powermobile days. Bug maven Lois Grace says that people everywhere enjoy seeing Beetles in competition alongside the more luxury-type cars. But, she stresses, it's not the prestige that attracts her to the Bug. It's love. "We have bought too easily into the theory the automotive industry itself has been busy shoving down our throats for years, that the 'lowly' VW is an economical car, and one not worthy of competing with the Big Guys. We need to stop selling ourselves short and stop helping to perpetuate the myth of the Bug being merely an affordable little car. We need to start thinking of it as the classic machinery that it is."

*Above: Two seashore Bugs emerge from the sand. Opposite: Beetles on a tree-lined country road in 1963.*

Everyone loves the Bug. Depending on whom you talk to, it's a blast from the past or an investment in the future. However, there are other viewpoints, especially those held by auto pundits who deem it their duty to break through the slanted subjectivity of fandom with objective opinions on the car. That doesn't always sit well with Beetle fans. Grace takes umbrage at the opinions of Tom and Ray Magliozzi, fondly known by their National Public Radio listeners as Click and Clack. In addition to their *Car Talk* program that airs every weekend, the entertaining car mechanics have a syndicated column that runs in newspapers across the U.S. They like to poke fun at the Beetle. This bugs Grace.

She's held a vendetta against Click and Clack ever since she read one of their columns in the *San Jose Mercury*. A young woman asked what type of burglar alarm they would recommend for her '65 Bug. They wrote back that a buying an alarm for it was like putting barbed wire around the kitty litter box. Grace growls and says, "Nothing chaps my hide faster than someone insulting my beloved auto."

Even on their own *CarTalk* Web site listeners lodge their objections to the Magliozzi brothers anti-Bug talk. One Beetle owner chastised them by writing, "I absolutely adore my car, and I'm getting kind of tired of you two chowderheads trashing VWs all the time! I mean, it's not like I have dependents counting on my not getting smooshed in an accident. Let me enjoy my little sardine can."

Kevin Berger is another opinionated car guy who has written two books on the cultural and the environmental impact automobiles have on our lives, *Zen Driving* and *Where the Road and the Sky Collide*. Berger, whose family owned a couple of Bugs, has a few theories as to why the car became so popular. He notes that when the Bug first appeared in America, none of the big three auto makers paid any attention to women or to people who were hip. But Volkswagen did. "The first stirrings of the women's move-

ment came when they began to do a lot of driving," he says. "That necessitated having an inexpensive second car to go along with the big family car. The Volkswagen Bug fit that need perfectly."

As for the hep aspect of the car, Berger cites the early marketing campaign, singling out the "My car is a lemon" ad. "It was not only self-deprecating but it also played on the notion that more and more American-made cars were being perceived as lemons. That ad appealed to hip audiences."

Berger also opines that the Bug generated a faithful following because it was relatively easy to fathom mechanically. You could become close to your car psychologically because you could understand it. "It was such a simple car to work on that people got attached to their Bugs."

However, Berger doesn't go easy on the car. He points out that the innocuous-looking little vehicle is a notorious polluter that spews out enough hydrocarbons to make the EPA shudder. That's why Beetles still manufactured in Mexico are outlawed on U.S. roadways. "New cars are extremely clean compared to the Beetle," he says. "Autoworkers in Detroit used to make fun of radical environmentalists driving around in them because the Bug was one of the worst polluters on the road."

In 1996, Sunny Andersen founded *Girlyhead*, a spin-off of the car magazine *Gearhead*. While her 'zine has a more expansive pop culture scope, it also includes coverage of auto issues. Partial to big American cars from the sixties, Andersen has never owned a Bug and vows to steer clear of one in the future. She grew up in San Francisco where, she says, "If you threw a stone in any direction you'd hit one." All of her friend's parents had Beetles, which meant that when she was growing up in the seventies she always had to squeeze into the back seat of one with several of her playmates. "The Bug was always loud so we couldn't talk to each other and it always shook. My parents had a Ford Galaxie

*Opposite: Who says the Bug doesn't have enough hauling capacity? A holiday tree just takes extra ingenuity and a little rope.*

*Bears love Bugs in Yosemite, top, and in Florida, above.*

convertible, which was so big it could fit three families. Beetles always made me feel claustrophobic."

As for the new Beetle, Andersen brands it a yuppie car even though she thinks it's adorable. Still, she couldn't see herself driving one. "If I owned a red round Beetle, I'd have to wear a red clown nose when I drove it," she says. "Recently I saw two guys my age driving one that was painted with all these hippie-dippy fall leaves. I guess it was meant to hearken back to the old hippie Bugs."

Anderson admits that the new Beetle is stylish in comparison to all the "cookie-cutter" models on the market and that owning one does make a statement against auto makers taking the safe, unimaginative design route. But she's still not tempted to purchase one. "I'd much rather buy a roomy, thousand dollar used Chevy that I can work on myself."

The Bug has a way of nudging itself not only into auto books and magazines, but has come alive in fiction as well. In his black-comedy novel *Still Life With Volkswagens*, British author and Beetle fan Geoff Nicholson digs below the sunny image of the Vee Dub to expose a burgeoning neo-Nazi movement in England that places Hitler's car on a pedestal. The 1995 book is a sequel to *Street Sleeper* (Sceptre Books, London), Nicholson's first novel published in Great Britain in 1987. In it, the author introduces several characters who later appear in *Still Life*. In the first book, the protagonist Barry Osgathorpe decides to quit his humdrum job as a librarian and hit the road as a Zen Road Warrior with the name Ishmael (as in *Moby-Dick's* "Call me Ishmael"). His transportation? A souped-up black Bug that he christens Enlightenment. Ishmael is no Mel Gibson. Don Quixote is more like it.

In *Street Sleeper*, Ishmael is a fool figure who becomes a valiant knight-errant, then almost as quickly gets reduced to the role of disgraced hero. At the beginning of *Still Life*, we find the disillusioned Barry has retreated in solitude to a trailer park with his black Beetle under wraps. However, because of a mysterious rash of exploding Beetles, Ishmael

When Apple Computer Inc. unveiled its new iMac computer on May 6, 1998, its rounded contour drew comparisons to the new Beetle, which had recently appeared on American streets. Mitch Mandich, Apple senior vice president for sales, likened the iMac to the new Beetle, describing the computer as an updated, more modern version of the old Bug. Market analyst Lou Mazzucchelli of Gerard Klauer Mattison gave the computer an enthusiastic thumbs-up, noting that people "have the same emotional reaction" to the iMac as they do to the new Beetle.

In an article on blimps ("Up, Up, and Away" in the *East Bay Express*), writer Jack Mingo suspects that the fascination with the airship has something to do with a primal imprinting of its shape. "Like other rounded bulbous things—Bugs, beagle puppies, statues of Buddha and very pregnant women, to name a few—blimps seem to inspire amused and indulgent smiles wherever they appear."

In April 1994, San Francisco Giants manager Dusty Baker explained why he gave his slumping superstar Barry Bonds a rare day off from playing. He said Bonds needed a mental day to think through his batting mechanics because his timing was off. "[Barry is] such a finely tuned machine. If you have a Volkswagen and the timing is off, it still runs OK. If it's a Ferrari and the timing's off, it runs like a tractor."

Back in the early days of the U.S. space program, the Volkswagen Beetle was used as a reference point for describing the newfangled technology. Crew engineers of the Gemini spacecraft described the living quarters of astronauts James McDivitt and Edward White, in orbit around the earth for four days, as the size of the front seat of a Volkswagen. For the same flight, Cape Kennedy spokesmen reported the first stage of the Titan engine generated four hundred thirty thousand pounds, roughly the equivalent thrust that would be produced by two hundred nineteen thousand Bugs.

because of a mysterious rash of exploding Beetles, Ishmael is called back to action. Through a series of comic incidents, Ishmael proceeds to break up a Vee Dub-driving band of punk terrorists led by the Hitler-loving character Phelan as well as inadvertently solves the case of the firebombed Bugs.

Nicholson's books are no Valentines to Beetles or their owners. In *Still Life*, he exposes the Bug's shadow. In addition to dredging up the specter of Hitler and other vile figures such as Charles Manson and Ted Bundy, Nicholson creates characters who are ambivalent at best when it comes to their assessments of the Beetle.

Before donning his Ishmael persona, Barry fantasizes about forming an eco-friendly VW club called the Green Beetles which has as its only membership requirement that the air polluting car never be driven. Fat Les, the Beetle guru who renovates and customizes Volkswagens, goes through a severe identity crisis that results in him resenting the car and wondering if there's more to life than a four-cylinder, air-cooled piece of machinery.

Former politician and mental ward patient Charles Lederer has Beetle phobia. He describes the car's engine as having a "horrid death rattle," subscribes to the philosophy that "wherever there's trouble, there's always a Volkswagen," and concludes that since the Beetle is the car of the Devil it must be destroyed.

Nicholson even interjects himself into the mix, recounting some of his own Bug tales and downplaying speculation that he's a Beetle fanatic. His fondness for the Volkswagen, he writes, is akin to Herman Melville's interest in white whales.

One of the top news correspondents in the automotive world, Paul A. Eisenstein, remembers well the Beetle's glory days. Even though he never owned one, the Detroit-based Eisenstein enjoyed watching the car putt-putting its way down the street. "My friends had Bugs and they loved them," he says. "But they always scared me. I knew some-

one who was in an accident and put his head through the windshield." Safety issues still figure prominently in his assessment of the car. It's short, doesn't corner well, has lousy brakes and isn't passenger friendly. Plus, the early models aren't highway friendly. In a crash, the crush space up front gives way instead of absorbing the impact. He recalls a Bill Cosby joke that a Beetle would lose a head-on collision with a dog.

Eisenstein likens the nostalgia for the Bug to childbirth. "A lot of people tend to forget the pain of the vehicle and remember its glory," he says. "Still, I miss them. I do love seeing them on the road. Whenever I'm in California, I'm always amazed by how many of them are still around."

What impresses Eisenstein most about the Bug is not so much the car itself, but what it represented. He remembers hanging out in Greenwich Village as a young hippie wanna-be and appreciating how the car was such a counterculture symbol. He laughs at how the hippie movement that advocated the do-your-own-thing doctrine bought into Bugmania so wholeheartedly. For a group of rebels who prided themselves in being so unique, there was plenty of conformity. "We all dressed alike, wearing silly bell bottoms and loud shirts," Eisenstein says, "and we all drove the same anti-establishment car. The Beetle was the four-wheeled equivalent to love beads."

As a car buff in his youth, Eisenstein was also charmed by the Bug's unpretentiousness. "It was the antithesis of the bigger-is-better American automobile philosophy at the time. The new cars were lathered with chrome. The Beetle was small and sprightly and wasn't built to be taken seriously. Detroit took itself incredibly seriously. The American car makers made you feel like you were missing out if you didn't buy the latest Belchfire 88 model. Volkswagen didn't go for the planned obsolescence guilt trip. If you didn't trade your old car in right away, Volkswagen assured you that you weren't any less of a person."

*Previous spread: Windblown Lady took in the salty smells of the bay, as Elizabeth Hart cruised her car, "Buglete," across the Golden Gate Bridge. Opposite: The Bug was the main squeeze for sixties coeds. Above: After the wedding this Mexican wrought-iron Beetle moved to the Stiftung AutoMuseum Volkswagen in Wolfsburg.*

*Sisters praise Bugs.*

"Sure, they were German-made, but they were the Sergeant Schultz of automobiles. Everyone knew they weren't dangerous. They put a smiling face on an otherwise horrific period of history."

Eisenstein says he is amazed at how long the Beetle run lasted. But in the end, he asserts, its biggest fans led to its demise. The Baby Boomers who loved the Bug also championed Ralph Nader who decried the auto industry building unsafe cars. The hippies driving smoke-spewing Bugs were the ones calling for the EPA to have more authority to push for and enforce new emissions standards. "The people who bought the Beetle grew sophisticated, but the Beetle didn't," Eisenstein says. "By the seventies, people were finally convinced that the Beetle was on the right path. But the car did not change with the times. It wasn't as fuel

efficient as the Japanese imports, and it couldn't go for tens of thousands of miles without a lot of maintenance. The days where you prided yourself with how big a tool chest you carried in your car were over."

Eisenstein ranks Volkswagen's failure to come up with an updated Bug sooner as one of the biggest fiascoes in automobile history. "After the Beetle went away so completely and unceremoniously in 1979, Volkswagen began a slow collapse in the U.S. It didn't want to be perceived as the Beetle company any longer, which was a mistake. It failed to see how ingrained into the culture the car was. Sales went from over six hundred thousand units to well under one hundred thousand before the company came around. It's my guess that the only reason Volkswagen didn't pull out of the American market was Teutonic pride."

*a*bove all, the Bug is a bundle of fun. Throughout its lifetime, the car has inspired many games.

### Beetle Cram

Back in the innocent college days of panty raids and campus hijinks, students bored with academics dreamed up new ways of entertainment. Seeing how many people could jam, cram, squeeze their way into a telephone booth became a favorite pastime. The Volkswagen Beetle represented a variation on that theme. Rules included students poking up through sunroofs, flopping out the rear motor hood and plunked into the front luggage compartment.

### Volkstote

Reportedly invented at Wayne State University in Detroit, Volkstote involved carrying a Bug a hundred feet, then driving back to the starting line with all carriers riding in the car. Groups of strong-armed types were able to achieve the feat in less than a half-minute. The game became very popular in Australia.

### Engine Pull

Made popular at Bug-ins and various Beetle meets, this game was a variation on Volkstote, but was much more mechanically challenging. Rather than toting the Bug, teams removed the motor (all it takes is four bolts), refit it and then drove across a finish line. The fastest times were in the two-and-a-half minute zone.

### Slug Bug / Punch Buggy

With fewer and fewer Volkswagen Beetles on the highways of America, this game increases in popularity with youngsters. There are variations in tallying scores. At its most basic, Slug Bug allows the first person spotting a Bug license to slug or punch a fellow player in the arm. In some areas where Beetles are rare, the game doesn't last long because of sheer boredom. Long family trips, however, can make for lots of sightings. The game can be especially bruising if played in Mexico (where Beetles are still built) or anyplace in California. Sisters Katherine and Eva Corrigan of New York City counted nine hundred bugs on a single weekend while on a family trip to Cancun (neither ended up black and blue). A less physical and perhaps saner version of the game involves counting the number of Bugs, with special colors and other considerations garnering extra points. For instance, a cheetah-print version that Genny McAuley spotted on a Santa Monica side street earned 50 points.

*Two American icons: Coca-Cola and the Bug.*

# Afterword

Having owned three Bugs, I have my own satchel of stories.

My life with a Bug began early in my high school senior year in 1971. I bought my very first car, a beige '61 Bug, off a VW dealer's lot. Everyone else around me had hot cars, big American tanks that flashed and squealed through my blue-collar western Massachusetts town with macho assertiveness. Those were the cheapo gasoline days, long before the small cars imported from Japan conquered the American automobile market. The reservoirs of petrol, we were told, were bottomless, and the romance with huge cars was still in high gear. Big and roomy and comfortable was the norm. So why did I opt for a fuel-efficient Bug, a tiny bubble of a tin can that threatened to make me the laughing stock of the town?

As I look back, I recognize that those rowdy and reckless senior year days were when I first began to bloom into an eccentric who took great joy in upending expectations placed upon me. I couldn't have articulated it back then, but in retrospect the only car I could have owned at the time was a Volkswagen Bug. I was striving to be myself, to be different from everyone else, to question all authority. Unconsciously I wanted my first car to reflect that. I had to have wheels that stood for something, that epitomized nonconformity, that mocked tradition. It was destined that I would be one of a handful of kids in my class to tool around in a Beetle.

But being a freaky rebel has its downside. For the two years I owned the car the heater never worked, thereby making winter driving extra hazardous and January necking in the tiny back seat a freezer affair. I dressed in several layers and used the windshield scraper both inside and out. (My father discovered the best method for defrosting the tiny front windshield on extra frigid mornings. He kept candles in the ashtray and lit one when he needed to melt the freezing ice off the glass so he could see.)

When I went off to college, my dad paid my insurance and used the '61 Bug as his funky drive-to-work vehicle. By the middle of its second winter, the rust had become so cancerous that the bottom was decaying. You could see through the floorboards to the road below. It was retired into my parents' woodsy backyard where it continued to be useful before it was eventually towed to the auto graveyard. My sister and younger brothers learned how to drive by maneuvering through the trees.

My dad also rigged up an old mattress spring to the back bumper of the Bug, strategically piled heavy flagstones on it and graded the large hole bulldozed in the backyard that eventually became the ice-skating pond. The aging Beetle proved to be a great workhorse. It remained a backyard fixture for another year, housing wasps, mice and a few hibernating snakes.

The Bug has a notorious reputation for being incredibly easy to rip off. My partner Evantheia tells the story of her shiny VW getting stolen years ago. It was found several days later in a vacant lot, stripped to the frame. A total loss.

My close call came one summer when a couple of school kids wedged open the passenger pilot window, hot wired the ignition but then couldn't figure out how to break the steering lock on my '74. That wasn't the first break-in. I've had my share. For awhile they were averaging nearly one per year. I lost my tools and toolbox (which I thought were cleverly hidden beneath the driver's seat) and on another occasion a bunch of clothes that I found the next day in a bundle a couple blocks away. Another time I lost vise grips and the jack. Once somebody not only broke into my car to get a watch with a broken wristband and a few dollar bills I kept in the ashtray for bridge toll, but the thief hung out long enough to smoke a couple of cigarettes which he stubbed out in the ashtray.

But none of those little robberies was as dramatic as my very first night in Berkeley in 1976 after just having driven my '69 Beetle cross-country from Massachusetts. I was staying at a crash pad near Peoples Park and had taken only my most valuable possessions inside for the evening. The next morning I discovered that my car had been broken into. Three things were taken: a camping hatchet, a six-inch long fishing knife and allergy pills. Nice welcome.

My entire life has been spent driving a Volkswagen Beetle, save for a short spell after I abandoned my corroding '69 Bug at a roadside used car dealer in San Martin, California, in 1977. I traded in my trustworthy but exhausted car as a down on a Datsun pickup, a true lemon. It exhibited major engine problems almost immediately, sprung a leak in its radiator and was slowly dying when a year later I worked out another trade with a local rancher: the truck for five hundred dollars and a pig fully butchered and dressed. I used the cash to make a down on the '74 sitting in a Hollister lot just waiting for me.

In the course of writing this book, I talked with dozens of Volkswagen Bug fans—former owners as well as those who still have one in their possession—who love reminiscing about the car. They remembered the times when even though everything else was breaking down in their lives, their Beetles were still running.

But I also observed that the Bug doesn't necessarily inspire nostalgic pinings. Few people want to return to the old days of scraping the frost off the inside of the windshield or cramming six people into one to go for a joyride. Thinking back on Bug-friendly times is more like recalling an era with a gentle fondness even if it wasn't all a fun cruise.

But to the countless Bug drivers, myself included, who justifiably have a warm spot in their hearts for the car, it's thanks for the memories.

Postscript: After my initial brief fling with the new Beetle from Volkswagen's press fleet, I buckled into my wobbly '74 and proudly took to the highway, albeit with that familiar fumy smell and weak acceleration power. But with Beetlemania in the air again, I became acutely aware of older Bugs like my own, making mental notes about color, dents and age. I also noticed other people doing the same.

Six months later when my old Bug began to cough horribly on my return ride from the Monterey Jazz Festival, I began to reconsider having a classic as my main mode of transportation for long hauls. After pulling over twice to let the Bug catch its breath, I made a vow, nursed it home, delivered it to my mechanic and got hit with a hefty charge for a new carburetor and distributor (the diseased parts were originals that lasted over one hundred seventy five thousand miles).

My vow? For the first time in my life I promised to buy a brand spanking new car. It was a no-brainer as far as what I would purchase. After visiting a couple of Volkswagen dealerships, I found what I was looking for: a rare silver bullet newby. It's not the same as the old Bug, but strangely it conjures up the spirit of the old timers.

Speaking of which, did I get rid of the '74? No way. Even though it sits outside now instead of in the garage, it's just a matter of time before I pull the trigger on replacing the window rubbers, getting the traces of body rust removed, repairing dented fenders and then treating the beauty to a new clementine paint job.

First loves always hold a special place in our hearts.

# Acknowledgments

In the early stages of *The Bug Book*, I had a conversation with a writing colleague, Owen Edwards, about my desire to tell the story of how the Volkswagen Beetle became an American icon. I'm grateful that he identified my mission: exploring the culture of the Bug.

I owe my biggest debt of gratitude to my partner Evantheia Schibsted, who not only endured my Bug thoughts and anxieties for over a year, but also helped whenever she found time in her busy writing schedule to dig into the nitty-gritty business of tracking down sources, researching information and making invaluable contacts. She was able to break through walls that had been impenetrable to me.

Thanks to my jazz journalist buddy Bill Minor, who penned the superb book *Monterey Jazz Festival: Forty Legendary Years*. Through Bill, I had the opportunity to meet his publishers Paddy Calistro and Scott McAuley. Paddy and I agreed that someday we'd discuss some book ideas I'd been contemplating. As we parted, she spied my orange '74 Beetle parked on the street and remarked that it would be fun to do a Bug book. We clicked. From then on, it was full Bug ahead.

Special thanks to my publishers' daughter Genny McAuley, whose fascination with Bugs played a crucial role in determining that *The Bug Book* would be a winner. And to David McAuley, for his fine photos. Also special appreciation goes to copy editor Jane Centofante and to the excellent design team of Linda Warren and Laura Mische of The Warren Group in Venice.

Friends provided great support. Wendy LaRiviere and Nancy Larson proved to be better than a professional clipping service, feeding me several articles on all forms of Beetle. Thanks to Derk Richardson, Stu Brinin, Michael Bloom, Frank Foreman, Andreas Jones and Laurie Zimmerman who told me stories, supplied me with photos from their private collections and passed on names of excellent resources.

Often there was a string of contacts. For example, Stu has a friend who went to high school with Rube, who was president of a Bug club in upstate New York back in the seventies. That's how I got connected with Terri Gerber, a.k.a. Rube, who sent me a photo from her high school yearbook. Terri then linked me to Bill Cooney, a great interviewee in Boston. The amazing twist is that Bill bought his '55 Beetle sight-unseen from someone I had already talked to, Jan Peters, the founder of the Golden Gate chapter of the Vintage Volkswagen Club of America in California. It's a funny thing how the Bug makes the world all that much smaller. Through the club, I came into contact with several great Bug enthusiasts who proved helpful, including Rick Spohn, Ray Schubert, Taylor Nelson, Scott Leatherman, Lois Grace, Roscoe Walker and Linda Kowalski, who went the extra mile in helping me track down information and photos.

Thanks to all the photographers who made this book possible and to those people who led me to important images, including Brad Rickman of the San Francisco Jazz Festival who alerted me to photographer Michael Piazza's great cover shot.

Special thanks go to Ken Shapiro of Precision Peoples Car Repair in Berkeley. Not only has he taken good care of my '74 Bug, but he let me borrow several photos and books from his shop.

Thanks to the following folks at Volkswagen of America: Tony Fouladpour, Jaime Mercier and Linda Scipioni. Thanks to Volkswagen of America ad agency Arnold Communications and the VIPs there: Fran Kelly, Paul Nelson and Leslie Goober. Special acknowledgment must be made to Eckberth von Witzleben, who rolled out the red carpet for me in Wolfsburg.

During those months when I was unplugged from writing about the music scene, I was able to track down more Beetle juice from my contacts in the biz. Thanks to Erik Filkorn, Diana Sergi, Marshall Lamm, Sam Molineaux, Susan Deneau, Merrilee Trost, and Dr. Jazz.

Thanks to Paul Wilner, editor of the *San Francisco Examiner Sunday Magazine* and his team, Joey Rigg, Zahid Sardar and Alison Biggar, who worked on my new Beetle-meets-old Bug article "Buggy Love," which jumpstarted this project.

Also thanks to Paul A. Klebahn, the *Bug Tales* man who often called me on his cell phone while on the road. He's become a long-distance Bug friend. My appreciation goes to Melissa and Jerry Jess who let me borrow VW ads from their extensive collection.

Gotta give it up for my parents Flip and Shirlie Ouellette. Out of the blue one day my dad (who took me to the VW dealer in Springfield, Massachusetts, to buy my first Bug) called to tell me he had just shot a roll of pictures of incapacitated Beetles at the Ludlow Auto Salvage yard. Along with a stack of photos, he sent the water color of broken Bugs that appears on the dedication page—painted by my mom. Thanks, too, to my bros Scooter, Peter and Dave and my sis Karie for their support and encouragement. Also thanks to the Schibsted family: Steve and Leslie and their kids Drew and Allie as well as Jim and Penny and their kids Jon, Julie and Laurie, who took her first ride in a real Slug Bug (my '74) while I was writing this.

I haven't seen him since 1972, but I've got to thank my old high school friend Dennis Page who let me drive his father's VW months before I got my license. Those illegal spins on the streets of Ludlow made me fall head over heels for the Bug.

Thanks to all those friends who encouraged me throughout: Mark Halper, Lisa Lipman, Wendy Kaufmyn, Greg Beshouri, Karen Carroll, Eric Forno, Randall Kline, Teresa Pantaleo, Colleen and Ricky Paretty, Doug Sorensen, Tim Childress, Wayne and Shavonne Saroyan, Sharon Stanbridge, and the Greving family, Jani and Warren and their four Bug-loving children, Brett, Justin, Robin and Graham.

And, last but not least, where would I be without writer-printer-publisher Clif Ross, my closest friend, who faithfully checked on my progress during our weekly coffee drinking hangs at Royal Coffee in Oakland. Thanks, Clif.

## Bibliography

Blank, Harrod. *Wild Wheels.* Petaluma, California: Pomegranate Artbooks, 1993.

Dalyrmple, Marya, ed. *Is The Bug Dead?* New York: Stewart, Tabori & Chang, 1982.

Fisher, Bill. *How to Hotrod Volkswagens.* Los Altos, California: HP Books, 1970.

Gelderman, Carol. *Henry Ford: The Wayward Capitalist.* New York, New York: Dial Press, 1981.

Lax, Eric. *Paul Newman: A Biography.* Atlanta, Georgia: Turner Publishing, Inc., 1996.

Muir, John. *How to Keep Your Volkswagen Alive: A Manual of Step-By-Step Procedures for the Compleat Idiot.* Santa Fe, New Mexico: John Muir Publications, 1969.

Nelson, Walter Henry. *Small Wonder: The Amazing Story of the Volkswagen Beetle.* Cambridge, Massachusetts: Robert Bentley, Inc., 1998.

Nicholson, Geoff. *Still Life With Volkswagens.* Woodstock, New York: Overlook Press, 1995.

Nicholson, Geoff. *Street Sleeper.* London, England: Sceptre Books/Hodder and Stoughton Ltd, 1994.

Prew, Clive. *VW Beetle.* New York: Smithmark Publishers, 1993.

Seume, Keith. *California Look VW.* Osceola, Wisconsin: Motorbooks International, 1995.

Seume, Keith. *VW Beetle: A Comprehensive Illustrated History of the World's Most Popular Car.* Osceola, Wisconsin: Motorbooks International, 1997.

Zeichner, Walter. *VW Beetle Convertible, Karmann Ghia, Rometsch, 1949-1980.* West Chester, Pennsylvania: Schiffer Publishing Ltd, 1989.

## Videography

*History of the Volkswagen.* West Long Branch, New Jersey: Domino Films/KULTUR, 1994.

*Wild Wheels.* El Cerrito, California: Zoom In Productions, 1992.

## Photo and Image Credits

The author and publisher thank the following contributors for use of images in this book:

Cover image and page 9 by Michael Piazza for the San
    Francisco Jazz Festival
Harold Adler: 116-117
AP/World Wide Photos: 13, 14, 126
Howard Brainen: 76-77
Stuart Brinin: 138
©Disney Enterprises, Inc.: 40-41, 42
Mark S. Erlebacher: 62-63
Gail Goodwin: 31
Lois Grace: 30, 65 (bottom)
Ken Kerzner, Budget Rent-A-Car of Beverly Hills:
    39 (right)
Anthony King / Elizabeth Hart: 130-131
Dave McAuley: 95, 96, 98, 127
Mercier-Wimberg: 109
Kathrin Miller: 68
John Muir Publications: 79
Dan Ouellette: 74 (top), 75, 88 (bottom), 89 (top), 96-97,
    104-105
Philip J. Ouellette, Jr.: 80
Shirlie Ouellette, original watercolor: 140
John Pearson: 74 (bottom), 81, 89 (bottom), 90-91
Yunus Peer: 65 (top)
Evantheia Schibsted: 137
Rick Spohn: 64

Stiftung AutoMuseum Volkswagen: 16-17, 21, 23, 24
    (top), 25, 28-29, 40-41, 45, 50-51, 52, 53, 54, 55, 56-
    57, 58, 59, 84, 85, 88 (top), 93, 99, 112-113, 114 (left),
    119 (top), 124, 125, 128, 132, 133, 135, 142
UPI/Corbis-Bettmann: 87, 92
Volkswagen AG: 2, 5, 7, 13, 24 (bottom), 34, 35, 67, 72,
    103 (top), 106, 108
Volkswagen of America, Arnold Communications:
    103 (bottom), 114 (right), 119 (bottom), 121
Zefa/Index Stock Imagery: 134

## More Sources for Bug Goodies

Bug Tales™ by Paul A. Klebahn and Gabriella Jacobs is
available for $12.95 from Oval Window Press, Cincinnati,
Ohio.; see http://www.bugtales.com or phone 513-956-
7456 for more information.

Melissa and Jerry Jess: Collectors of Volkswagen Toys,
Literature, Memorabilia, Cars and Accessories in Phoenix,
Arizona can be reached on the Web at http://www.
mindspring.com/~deasterw/jess/jess.html or by phone at
602-867-7672.

*How to Keep Your Volkswagen Alive : A Manual of Step-By-
Step Procedures for the Compleat Idiot* is available from
John Muir Publications, Santa Fe, New Mexico; phone
800-888-7504.

*Wild Wheels* book or video is available from Harrod
Blank, 2248 Summer Street, Berkeley, California 94709;
e-mail excentrix@aol.com.